Patchwork
Made Easy

Peigi Martin & Susan Young

Sterling Publishing Co., Inc.   New York

Contents

Photography—Judith Long and Alan Gillard
Illustrations—Astrid Mensink
Design—Nick Charalambous

Published in the United States of America in 1988
by Sterling Publishing Co., Inc.
Two Park Avenue, New York, N.Y. 10016
First published in Australia © 1986
by Little Hills Press
Distributed in Canada by Oak Tree Press Ltd.
% Canadian Manda Group, P.O. Box 920, Station U
Toronto, Ontario, Canada M8Z 5P9
All rights reserved
Sterling ISBN 0-8069-6860-5 Paper
Sterling ISBN 0-8069-6882-6 Trade

Printed in Singapore

Introduction

Patchwork, an old craft as modern as today. A skill for those who enjoy artistry, technique, history, economy, design, practicality and fashion. These are the many aspects of patchwork making it suited to the needs of many who may want work as varied as an heirloom bedcover, an interpretative wallhanging, smart tablemats or a stylish carrybag.

In this book the numerous types, patterns and items of patchwork are photographed and clearly set out with easy-to-follow, detailed diagrams and instructions.

The Story of Patchwork

Patchwork probably dates back as far as clothing itself. The first patches were no doubt applied as a means of extending the life of a worn garment, though little evidence of the origins of patchwork and quilting has survived because the textiles were perishable.

A few very old examples have been discovered. A funeral tent canopy was found in the tomb of Queen Esi-mem-Kev of Egypt, who lived about 980 BC. It was made of gazelle hide with various applied designs.

Quilted garments seem to have been worn even earlier than this. A carved ivory figure of a Pharaoh of the Egyptian First Dynasty c. 3400 BC, discovered in 1903, depicts the Pharaoh wearing what seems to be a quilted mantle.

During the Middle Ages, quilted apparel was widely used for military wear. A well known surviving example is the Black Prince's quilted surcoat which used to hang above his tomb in Canterbury Cathedral.

The earliest surviving bed quilts are three of Sicilian origin, thought to have been made in 1395. One of these is in the Victoria and Albert Museum and is in extremely good condition, considering it is nearly 600 years old.

Pieced work did not become widespread until the 17th and 18th centuries when cotton printed fabrics from India became available. For the early American settlers in particular, fabric was extremely precious because English laws prevented the colonists from manufacturing their own or buying any cloth from anywhere but England. Because the fabric was so precious, early designs were based on simple shapes which wasted little fabric.

Patchwork quilting flourished from 1775 to 1830, then for a time it was regarded as the poor relation of other types of needlework, fit only for young girls learning to use a needle, and for old ladies with failing eyesight. Then from 1890 to 1940, there was an upsurge of interest, and many newspapers and magazines carried quilt patterns. During the 1950s and 1960s the popularity of quiltmaking declined.

In the 1970s there began the revival of interest which shows no sign of abating today.

We are fortunate to be making quilts in these times when we do it as a leisure activity, as a craft from which we gain pleasure and with a wide range of fabrics and equipment available.

Masterpiece quilts were the "best" quilts made by a woman who had had years of experience making utility quilts. *Masterpieces* were probably worked on only during daylight, and when the woman was rested.

Don't feel too discouraged if you see one of these exquisite quilts and compare it with your own efforts. Many more *Masterpiece* quilts have survived than everyday quilts, because they were reserved for the guestroom where they received little wear.

Equipment and Materials

Equipment

Although times have changed vastly since the first American quilts were made in the 17th century, today quilts and patchwork items are still made with the same basic tools. In other words, materials, needles, thread, pins and scissors. However, our great-grandmothers would surely have envied us our wonderful array of additional aids.

Needles

For piecing and quilting, a "between" needle is considered best. When a longer needle is required, a "sharps" needle is generally used. A No. 7 to No. 10 is recommended, but a good general rule is to use as fine a needle as you can manage comfortably.

Thread

One of the many recent improvements is the polyester core-wrapped thread, available in every imaginable colour. It is very strong and durable, but has a tendency to fray and tangle. This can be largely avoided by knotting the end before unrolling the thread, then cut and thread the other end through the needle. This idea is equally useful when dealing with other types of thread.

Until recently it was possible to obtain quilting thread in black or white, but a variety of shades is now available.

Pins

Glass headed pins are very sharp and are therefore excellent for piercing straight through the material when lining up a seam or a starting point.

A longer pin is available. This is particularly suitable for pinning together layers for more bulky projects.

Scissors

Today, a great variety of excellent quality scissors is available. They come in a wide range of shapes and sizes. It is important to make sure that scissors cut as well at the points as they do in the middle of the blades.

Cutters

Scissors will always be needed. However, an invaluable new addition to cutting aids is the Olfa Rotary cutter. A special mat to use with it is available. This makes it possible to accurately cut several layers of fabric at a time.

Rulers

An absolute "must" to use with the Olfa cutters is the long transparent ruler. It is well marked and very sturdy, so there is no danger of shaving off a piece of the ruler when cutting layers of fabric.

The photgraph also shows another ruler which is equally valuable when marking fabric with templates and seam allowances. This one is shorter and lighter, and is marked off in squares.

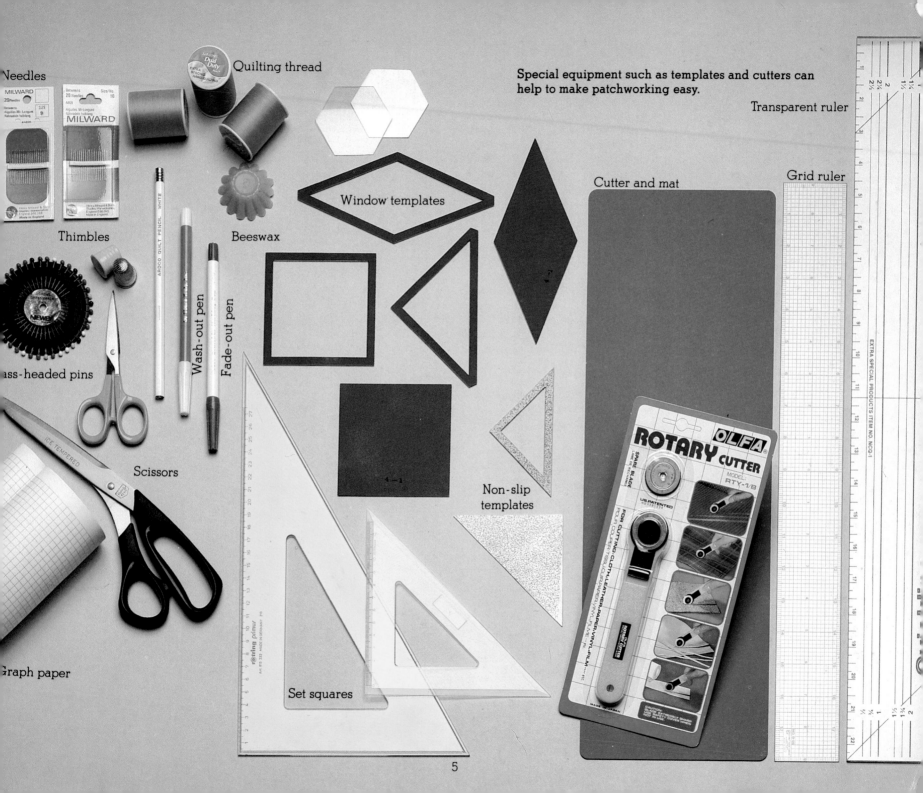

Needles

Quilting thread

Special equipment such as templates and cutters can help to make patchworking easy.

Transparent ruler

Thimbles

Beeswax

Window templates

Cutter and mat

Grid ruler

Wash-out pen

Fade-out pen

ass-headed pins

Scissors

Non-slip templates

ROTARY CUTTER OLFA

Graph paper

Set squares

5

Pencils

Whereas a soft lead pencil was once the only option for marking design and seam lines, a variety of marking pencils is now on the market. The water soluble one is probably the most used today.

Another very useful pencil is one that fades after a time. Be careful not to spend a lot of time marking more than you will have time to sew, because the design is liable to have disappeared by the time you get back to it.

Graph Paper

This is necessary when creating new designs or for altering the size of the old ones.

A tremendous help when working with diamonds and triangles, isometric graph paper can be purchased from most stationers.

Templates

Templates come in a great variety of shapes and sizes: solid templates, window templates made in metal or transparent plastic. These are virtually indestructable, which is an advantage when you compare with home-made cardboard ones. Cardboard is fine if the template is going to be used only a few times, but if a patch has to be cut out many times, the edges tend to wear out, resulting in inaccuracies. If you are embarking on a large project and using cardboard for templates, be prepared to cut out several of each shape being used.

Window templates are especially useful when a particular part of a fabric is being featured, when a flower or motif is to be centred in a patch.

Thimbles

It is a good idea to make a habit of using a thimble, especially if a quilt is the project on hand. As well as a metal thimble for the middle finger, a leather thimble used on a finger underneath the work to push the needle back up through the fabric saves many a sore finger.

Wax

If you keep a small piece of beeswax in your work box, you will be surprised how often you use it. As well as strengthening the thread, it makes it much easier to pull through the fabric.

Frames and hoops

It is not absolutely necessary to use a frame or hoop when quilting a small item, but a very much better finish will result if one is used. A frame or hoop will hold the three layers together and avoid any bunching up of the underneath layers.

Hoops come in a variety of shapes and sizes. A quilting hoop differs from an embroidery hoop in that it is deeper in order to accommodate the three layers of top, batting and backing. Some hoops come with a stand, leaving both hands free to work.

A quilting frame makes it very much easier to quilt large projects, such as quilts. Ideally the frame should be as wide as the project being quilted, but again, frames can be purchased in a variety of sizes or made by the home handyman.

Materials

Choice of a suitable fabric type is very important, especially for a beginner, because some fabrics are so much easier to work with than others. Some fabrics which are difficult to handle such as silk, velvet or wool can be used for patchwork and can look stunning, but don't choose them for your first project.

The best fabric to begin with is a firmly woven, lightweight, pure cotton, but many polyester cotton blends are quite manageable.

You will learn to read the label on the bolt or roll of material, to check the composition of the fabric, and to assess its suitability by handling it. If your project is to be hand quilted, avoid stiff, hard or heavyweight materials, as they will be almost impossible to quilt.

Experience will teach you which fabrics are a joy to use and which are an absolute headache. Very thin, sheer fabrics are a problem because the seams show through from the front, but if you have found the perfect colour or design in such a fabric it can be used if it is lined with a lightweight fabric. All the fabrics chosen for a particular project should be of similar weight.

Choice of Print

Many small scale floral prints are available. They are a safe choice for patchwork. However, they can sometimes be so safe and so well colour-coordinated that they result in a rather dull and uninspired finished effect. Experiment with prints of varying scale, stripes and border designs, geometric prints and checks. Some large scale prints can introduce a delicate, lacy effect. Particular care must be taken with stripes because if they are not cut and sewn perfectly straight, it will be very obvious.

When deciding which fabric to use, it often helps to stand back and view them from a distance. If your design depends on a light/dark colour scheme, make sure there is contrast between the fabrics. Skill in combining fabrics effectively is what makes one quilter's work stand out from another's, even though the workmanship may be equal.

The techniques of sewing patchwork are easily mastered, but the skill of working with fabrics is acquired only with experience. It is very helpful to study quilting books and magazines, and analyse the quilts pictured. Ask yourself why some quilts appeal to you more than others, how a particular effect has been achieved, and observe the effect of different colour schemes.

Fabric Quantities

It is useful to draw up your entire design. Use the drawing to count the number of pieces of each shape required. Then you can calculate how many of each piece can be cut from one width of 45 inch (115 centimetre) wide fabric. This information is used to work out the amount of material required. For example, if eight pieces can be cut from one width, and you need a total of 80 pieces, 10 rows will have to be cut. If the height of the piece is 4 inches (10 centimetres), allow 5 inches (12 centimetres) for cutting.

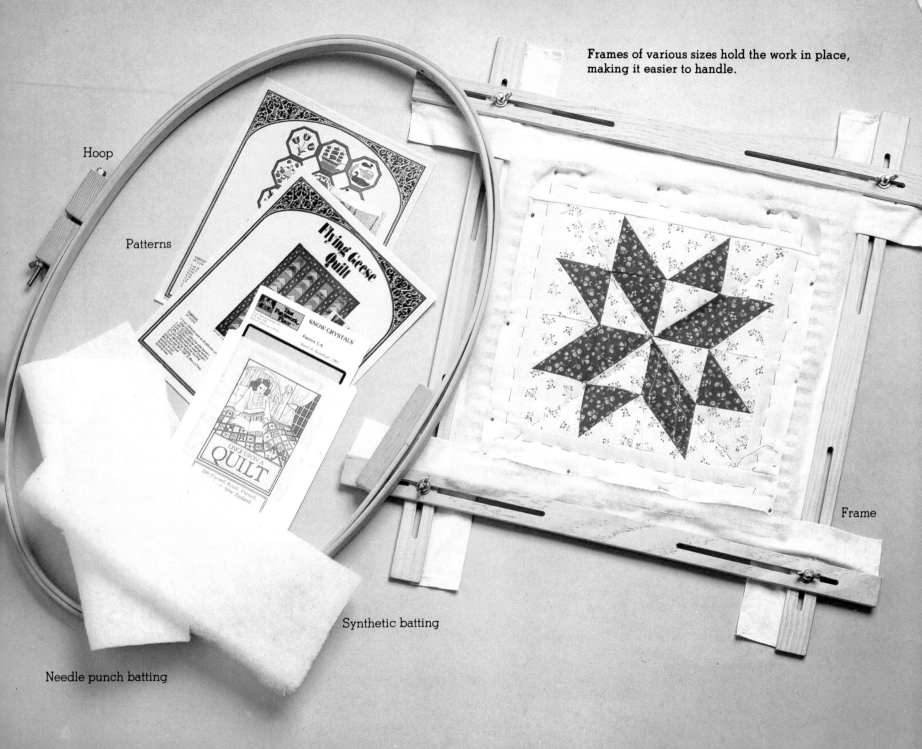

Frames of various sizes hold the work in place, making it easier to handle.

Hoop

Patterns

Needle punch batting

Synthetic batting

Frame

You will need 1½ yards (1.20 metres) of 45 inch (115 centimetre) wide fabric. That is 8 x 10 = 80 pieces; 10 rows by 5 inches = 50 inches, so you will need to buy 1½ yards; 10 rows x 12 centimetres = 120 centimetres = 1.20 metres.

It is a good idea to buy a little extra as insurance against cutting mistakes or mistakes in working out how much fabric you need. Any excess is useful in building up a collection of scrap fabrics for other projects.

Preparation

Always wash your fabrics before use. This will pre-shrink them, remove excess dye and remove any sizing, making the fabric easier to handle. Machine washing is good, unless you have a very small quantity of fabric.

The volume of water used seems to flush the dye and sizing out thoroughly. Problems are unusual, with the dye running from one fabric to others, but if you are suspicious of a fabric it would be wise to handwash it separately. If using the tumble dryer, a very short time is sufficient, unless the pieces are very large. Be careful not to over-dry the fabrics, as they may become very creased. It is better to remove them while they are still slightly damp, and then iron them.

Batting

This is the padding that plumps up the quilt. It goes between the top and the backing. Modern quiltmakers generally use the synthetic battings which are wide-ly available from specialist patchwork shops and also from dress fabric shops that cater for the quilter. Synthetics have many advantages: they are light yet warm and easy to handle; they are also stable and washable.

Several weights are available. A thin, lightweight batting is ideal for hand quilting, because it is much easier to produce small, even stitches.

It also gives a more authentic appearance to traditional quilt designs. However, the thicker battings are useful if you want extra warmth. They can be tied rather than quilted.

Old quilts were made using a variety of fillings — flannel sheeting, worn quilts or scraps from clothing, or a woollen or cotton batting. The cotton was particularly unstable and tended to redistribute itself, forming lumps, after washing. For this reason, quilts with a cotton filling had to be very closely quilted. If you examine pictures of old quilts, you will see that in addition to the decorative motifs, the background was also quilted. This must have been immensely time consuming. The major advantage of the synthetic battings is that they do not require nearly as much quilting.

Another type of batting is called needlepunch batting and can be purchased from dress fabric shops. It is a thin, firm batting, not suitable for quilts, but very useful for wall hangings, placemats or quilted clothing.

Construction and Finishing

Methods of Joining Blocks

Blocks joined edge-to-edge:
Join the blocks to form strips the width of the quilt, then sew the strips to each other to form the quilt top. Pin each seam very carefully, inserting a pin wherever seams meet, at right angles to the seam. Stitch right up to the pin and insert the machine needle at that point before removing the pin, then continue stitching.

Blocks joined with vertical and horizontal sashing:
Join the blocks into strips with a vertical sash between each pair of blocks. Sew a horizontal piece of sashing to each strip, then join the strips to form the quilt top.

(See Fig. 1,1a)

Borders

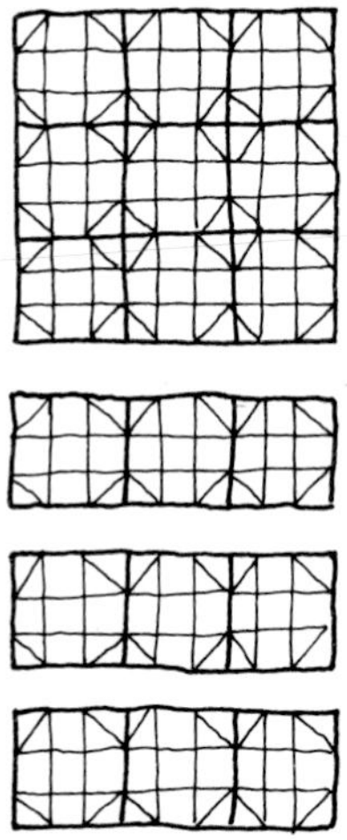

Borders are added to the quilt top after it has been assembled. Not all quilts require borders, but they often frame the design and look most attractive, especially if enhanced by quilting. They are also useful to increase the size of the quilt without making additional blocks.

A series of two or more borders can also be used, generally using fabrics which are in the quilt. When adding more than one border, the appearance will be more pleasing if they are of different widths. Borders should be cut from the length of the fabric before cutting the pieces for the

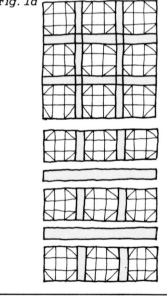

Fig. 1

Fig. 1a

quilt from that fabric, as seams in the borders should be avoided. If really necessary printed fabrics can be pieced without noticeable seams, but plain borders should not have any seams.

Fig. 2

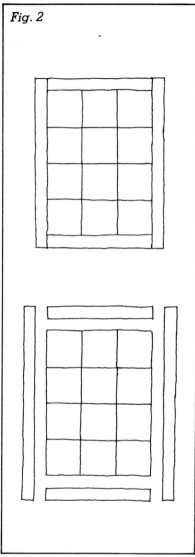

Square Corner Border

Cut two border strips equal in length to the width of the quilt. Sew these to the top and bottom of the quilt. Trim the borders even with the quilt sides. Press. Cut two more border strips equal in length to the length of the quilt plus the top and bottom borders.

Sew these strips to the sides of the quilt. Trim off the excess length, then press.

(See Fig. 2)

Mitred Borders

A mitred border is not difficult, and it gives a very professional finish. Cut four border strips, allowing extra length to form the mitre. Sew one strip to each side of the quilt, leaving excess at each end. Begin and end the stitching ¼ inch (6 millimetres) from the edge of the quilt. Lay the quilt flat. Fold each border and press so a crease is formed, beginning where the stitching stopped, and ending at the outer edge of the border strip. Match the two creases, and stitch, keeping the seam allowances free. Trim the excess and press. Repeat at each corner.

(See Fig. 3,3a,b,c)

Squared Corners

Sew a border strip to the top and bottom edges, and trim even with the sides. Cut from a contrasting fabric a square the same width as the border. Sew this to the border strip. Then sew it to the side of the quilt, matching the seam of the square to the border seam on the top edge of the quilt. Stop sewing a short distance from the lower border, and trim level with the border seam plus a ¼ inch (6 millimetre) seam allowance. Sew a square to the lower end of the border, then continue sewing it to the quilt. Repeat on the other side.

(See Fig. 4,4a,b,c)

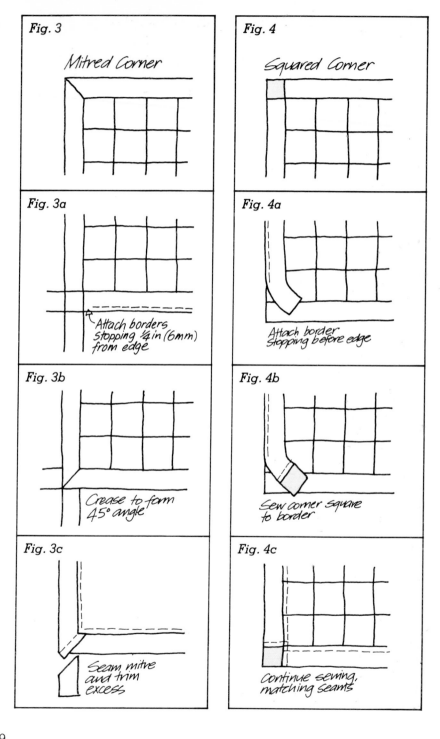

Assembling the Layers

The finished quilt is made up of three layers: backing fabric, the batting and the quilt top. These layers must be basted together securely before the edges are finished and the quilting done. This is often the most tedious part of the quilt making, but it is most important and is well worth the effort of doing it well. Any wrinkles that are allowed to creep in at this stage will be permanent.

Backing

A sheet is ideal for the backing as it will be large enough without requiring any joins. Calico or lining fabric are also suitable. Trim off the selvedges, then join the backing pieces and press the seams open. Make sure the backing is at least 4 inches (10 centimetres) larger than the quilt top on all sides. Lay the backing face down on a large carpeted area. Secure all round with pins. Use heavy-duty pins which are longer and thicker than dressmaking pins, inserting them through the fabric and into the carpet at an angle.

Batting

Polyester or needle punch batting is available in a variety of widths and thicknesses. For a full-sized quilt it will usually require joining — simply butt the edges together and whipstitch.

Quilting thread is ideal for this as it is light but strong. Spread the batting out on top of the backing.

Quilt Top

Trim all stray threads as they may show through the lighter fabrics. Press the top thoroughly and lay on top of the batting. Pin the quilt top in the same way as the backing; it should be stretched very slightly so there are no wrinkles but it should not be taut. If you can persuade someone to help you, it is much easier with two people working from opposite sides.

(See Fig. 5)

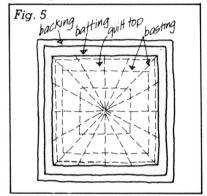

Fig. 5 backing batting quilt top basting

Basting

Use quilting thread in a contrasting colour to baste the quilt. Because it is strong, it will hold the layers securely and will be easy to remove once the quilting is finished. Start at the centre and work out to each side, then work diagonal lines. Next, baste parallel to the edges, one or two lines, depending on the size of the quilt. Finally, baste round the outside 8 to 12 inches (20 to 30 centimetres) in from the edge. Baste slowly and carefully so the layers remain smooth and without wrinkles. Remove the pins, and trim excess backing and batting level with the quilt top.

Finishing the Edges

There are several ways to finish the edges of your quilt. A bias bound edge is the most professional and durable. The edges of the quilt will receive the most wear, so it makes sense to finish them as securely as possible. For this reason, a double thickness bias binding for all bed quilts is used, but single binding is sufficient for wall quilts.

It is a good idea to finish the edges as soon as the layers have been basted together, because the quilting proceeds more easily without raw edges and loose threads. Also it is a boost to have the edges finished so the quilt is ready for use as soon as the quilting is finished.

Bias Binding

To Cut Bias Strips

Fold the fabric on the true bias by lining up the cut edge with the selvedge. Fold again, matching the folds. Mark the fabric into strips of the desired width, starting at the fold. Cut into strips. Sew the strips together to form one long strip. Press the seams open. For a double binding, fold the strip in half lengthways, and press.

For single binding, cut strips four times the desired finished width. For double binding, cut strips six times the desired finished width.

(See Fig. 6a,b,c)

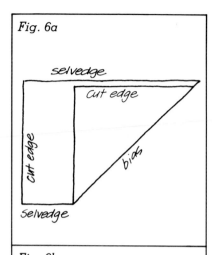

Fig. 6a selvedge cut edge cut edge bias selvedge

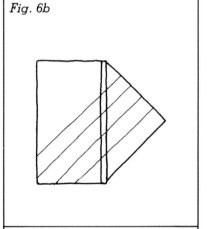

Fig. 6b

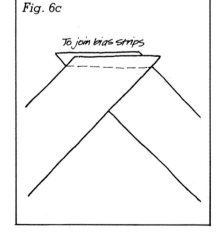

Fig. 6c To join bias strips

Fig. 6d

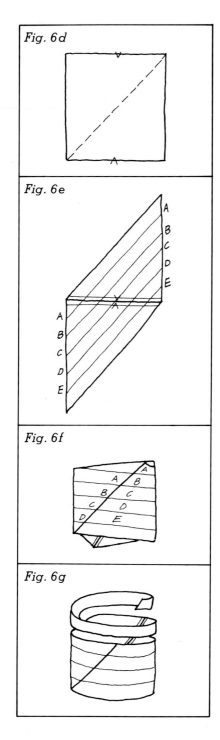

Fig. 6e

Fig. 6f

Fig. 6g

To Make Continuous Bias

Cut a large square of fabric. Mark the centre on opposite edges. Fold in half diagonally, and press lightly. Cut apart on the fold line. Join the two triangles, matching the centre marks. Press the seam open, and mark strips parallel to the diagonal cut. Seam the edges, with the strip marks offset by one width, as shown. Cut along the marked lines to form one continuous bias strip. For double bias, fold in half lengthways, and press.

(See Fig. 6 d,e,f,g)

To Attach Bias Binding

Pin the binding to the quilt top, beginning in the centre of one side and leaving 6 inches (15 centimetres) free. Stitch the binding to the quilt with a ½ inch (12 millimetre) seam, stopping ½ inch (12 millimetres) from the edge. Backstitch, and snip the threads.

Fold the binding to the right, at right angles to the seam, forming a diagonal fold. Press the fold lightly, and fold the binding forward, aligning it with the adjacent edge of the quilt. Begin stitching again at the raw edge and continue to the next corner. Repeat the process.

When you have almost reached the binding that was left free at the beginning, stop stitching and remove the work from the machine. Seam the ends of the binding, then finish stitching it to the quilt.

Press the binding away from the quilt top and fold it over the raw edge to the back. A mitre will

form on the front at each corner. Fold the binding so another mitre forms on the back. Slipstitch the binding to the back of the quilt, taking a few stitches in each mitre to hold it in place.

(See Fig. 7a,b)

Fig. 7a

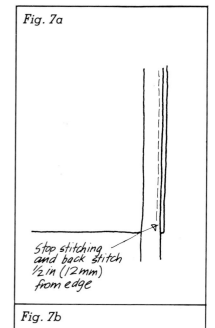

Stop stitching and back stitch ½ in (12mm) from edge

Fig. 7b

Form diagonal fold

Fig. 7c

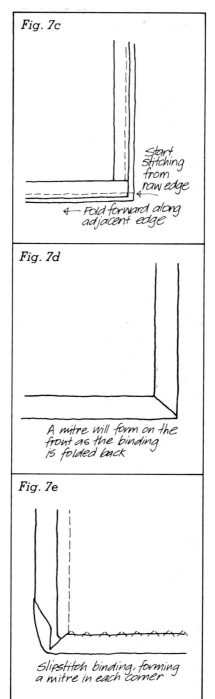

Start stitching from raw edge

← Fold forward along adjacent edge

Fig. 7d

A mitre will form on the front as the binding is folded back

Fig. 7e

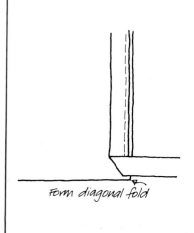

Slipstitch binding, forming a mitre in each corner

Quilting

Once the layers of the quilt have been assembled, basted securely and the edges bound, you are ready to begin quilting. The quilting has a dual role: it is functional because it holds the layers together and strengthens the quilt, and it is decorative because the stitches emphasise the pieced design or create their own independent design. The quilting adds an extra dimension to the finished appearance. Hand quilting, which is used in nearly all projects in this book, is also a pleasant and relaxing pastime. It has a soft, smooth and unwrinkled finish which cannot be equalled by machine quilting.

(See Fig. 8)

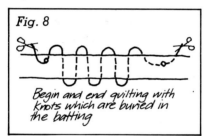
Fig. 8
Begin and end quilting with knots which are buried in the batting

Hand quilting uses a simple running stitch. The stitches should be small, even and straight. Concentrate at first on making the stitches even and straight. They will become smaller as you become more proficient. You will probably find it easier to work either toward yourself or from right to left.

To begin quilting, thread the needle and knot the end of the thread. Insert the needle through the top layer about ¾ inch (2 centimetres) from the starting point and

bring it up at the starting point. Tug gently on the thread so the knot is pulled through the top layer and becomes lodged between the layers. With one hand on top, push the needle down through all the layers. With the other hand underneath, feel the needle and return it to the top.

Continue with a gentle rocking motion, picking up several stitches at a time. The space between the stitches should be the same length as the stitches. End a line of stitching by knotting the thread, taking the last stitch and tugging the knot through the top layer. Bring the needle up a short distance away, and cut the thread close to the surface.

Hints for Successful Quilting

Don't make the mistake of thinking that quilting will be more effective if you use a thick, puffy batting. The lightest batting will be equally effective and considerably easier to work on.

When working on several parallel lines, have a needle threaded for each line, and work with each in turn until you are ready to change direction or move onto a new area.

(See Fig. 9)

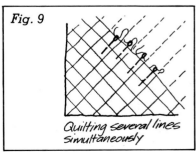
Fig. 9
Quilting several lines simultaneously

Avoid unnecessary stops and starts by planning the direction of stitching of a motif. Move to a nearby motif by running the needle under the top layer, rather than ending the stitching and starting afresh.

Quilting Designs

The most common of the traditional designs is known as outline quilting. Each piece is quilted ¼ inch (6 millimetres) in from the seamline.

(See Fig. 10)

Another method is to outline a particular shape in the design, rather than each piece.

(See Fig. 11)

If the quilt has alternate plain blocks or other plain areas, they are the ideal place for a more elaborate quilted motif.

(See Fig. 12)

Marking Quilting Designs

Outline quilting does not require marking, because a line ¼ inch (6 millimetres) in from the seamline can be judged by eye, though you may wish to mark this line for your first attempts.

Straight line designs can be marked with dressmakers' chalk, pencil, fade-out pen, wash-out pen or pencil (pages 4 to 6) and a ruler.

Ornamental motifs can be marked with a template or a stencil that you can buy or make at home.

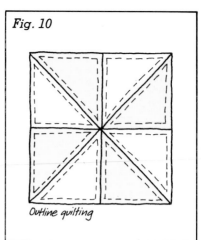
Fig. 10
Outline quilting

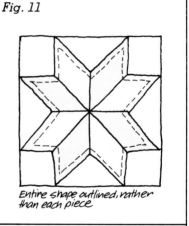
Fig. 11
Entire shape outlined, rather than each piece

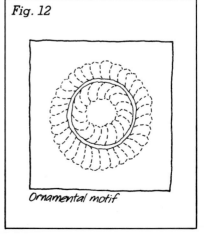
Fig. 12
Ornamental motif

Quilt Construction

Quilts may be pieced by hand or by machine. Both methods have advantages and disadvantages, and some techniques are better suited to one method than the other. It is a good idea to become adept at both hand and machine piecing so you can choose the most suitable method for a particular project. The major advantages of machine sewing are speed and strength, making it ideal for items which will receive a lot of wear and require frequent washing. It is not as suitable for intricate piecing involving curves or sharp angles. Long hours spent at the sewing machine can be tedious as it is not possible to converse or listen to the radio over the noise of the machine.

Hand piecing is much more time-consuming than machine sewing, but it has many advantages. It is portable and can be done while travelling or waiting for appointments or while waiting for children at sports events or music lessons. It is also more sociable as it can be done while talking to friends or family and is a worthwhile alternative to eating while watching television.

How to Hand Piece

Decide before cutting whether you intend to piece by hand or machine, because different cutting techniques and templates are used. For hand piecing, the sewing line must be marked on the fabric. Use a template which is finished size, and mark around it onto the fabric. Cut out, allowing ¼ inch (6 millimetre) seam allow-ance (judge this by eye). Sew the pieces together, matching the sewing lines. A window template can also be used to enable you to mark both sewing and cutting lines.

Place the pieces to be joined, right sides together, and stitch along the sewing line with a running stitch. Knot the thread, and secure the beginning and ending with a backstitch.

Press the seams to one side, usually to the darker side. This is stronger than pressing the seams open.

Machine Piecing

For machine piecing, use templates which include a ¼ inch (6 millimetre) seam allowance. Mark around the template onto the fabric. This is the cutting line. It is not necessary to mark the sewing line, because the edge of the presser foot is aligned with the cut edge of the fabric. On most machines this will give you an accurate ¼ inch (6 millimetre) seam allowance. If your machine is different, use masking tape to mark a guide line on the throat plate of the machine.

Machine piecing will go much more smoothly if you give some thought to a logical joining sequence. All the small units should be joined to form larger units, which are in turn joined to form the block.

Chainsewing is a great time saver. Instead of removing each unit from the machine and cutting the threads, simply feed the units through the machine one after the other without cutting the threads, until all the pieces have been joined. Then cut the units apart, press the seams to one side, and assemble the next stage in the same manner. It is not necessary to backstitch, as each seam will be crossed by another.

When joining pieces where seams must meet, pin accurately with the pin inserted into the seamlines at right angles to the line to be sewn. Sew right up to and over the pin so the fabric does not get a chance to move before it is stitched. This can be rather hard on your machine needle, so remember to replace it frequently.

Tied Quilts

Tying is an alternative method of holding the layers of a quilt in place. It is quicker than quilting, and in some cases is the only practical method. For example, if a very thick batting has been used for extra warmth, the thickness makes quilting very difficult so you may prefer to tie the quilt. Patchwork done with heavyweight materials or onto a backing square may also be better tied than quilted.

The layers of the quilt must still be basted together (Page 18). The ties may be positioned according to the patchwork design, or it may be necessary to mark evenly spaced points on the quilt top.

Traditionally, the ties were visible on the top surface of the quilt for added decoration.

To Form Ties

Thread a larger-eyed needle with a strong decorative thread such as acrylic yarn, crochet or but-tonhole thread or embroidery cotton. Make a stitch from the top through all layers and back to the top, leaving a length of thread to form the tie. The stitch may be repeated for extra strength. Knot the thread ends securely, and trim, leaving a tail about ¾ inch (2 centimetres) long. Tufts can be formed by using two or three strands instead of a single thread.

If you wish to tie a quilt but do not want to have visible knots or tufts, you may prefer to work from the backing side and form the knots on the underside so only the small stitch will show on the top. For barely visible ties which are still secure, use a matching shade of quilting thread, and position the stitches in seamlines, then tie on the underside. This method was used for the Log Cabin Cot Quilt (Page 42).

An alternative to ties is to stitch buttons at regular intervals over the quilt top.

Cushions

For a tailored look, finish the cushions with piping. You can use bought piping or make your own by cutting bias strips wide enough to cover the cording, plus seams (Page 19). Using a zipper foot, stitch next to the cording. Sew the piping to the cushion front, with the piping just inside the seam line. Clip the seam allowance of the piping at the corners, and slightly round the corners. Finish the ends of the piping by opening one end and overlapping the fabric.

(See Fig. 1)

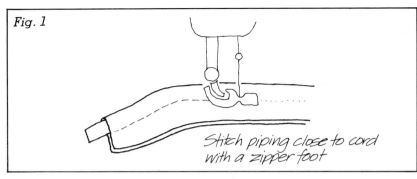

Fig. 1

Stitch piping close to cord with a zipper foot

Cut the backing ½ inch (1 centimetre) larger than the front. After attaching the piping, pin the backing to the front, right sides together. Sew with the wrong side of the front uppermost, so the previous stitching line is visible. Stitch, using the zipper foot, a little closer to the piping so the previous stitching will not show on the right side. Leave an opening for turning and filling. Close by slipstitching.

(See Fig. 2)

An alternative method is to use two overlapping pieces for the backing, and make a separate case for the cushion filling which is inserted into the cushion cover. This has the advantage of being easily removed for washing, and the inserts can be rotated among several covers for variety.

Cut two backing pieces, each two-thirds of the finished size. Hem one edge of each piece, and overlap the hemmed edges. Machine baste the overlapped edges. Pin to the cushion front, right sides together, and stitch right round the outer edge. Turn through the opening between the overlapped edges.

(See Fig. 3)

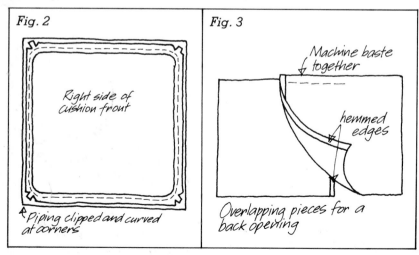

Fig. 2

Right side of Cushion front

Piping clipped and curved at corners

Fig. 3

Machine baste together

hemmed edges

Overlapping pieces for a back opening

Care of Quilts

Having lavished hours of work on making a quilt, you will obviously want to care for it in the best possible manner, as it may become an heirloom of the future. Here are some suggestions which will help to prolong its life.

Firstly, while using and enjoying your quilt, try to minimise the amount of wear and tear it receives. It is a good idea to get into the habit of folding back the quilt at night so it lies across the foot of the bed only. Or remove it entirely. In this age of electric blankets and heated waterbeds, the quilt is often decorative rather than functional and receives less wear. If you do require the quilt for warmth at night, use a sheet under it, which can be turned back over the top edge of the quilt, extending at least a yard (1 metre) towards the foot of the bed. This will greatly reduce soiling. The sheet can easily be washed as often as required. Quilts made from suitable fabrics can be washed very successfully, but it is still worthwhile caring for the quilt so it does not need frequent washing.

Sunlight will weaken the fibres of the fabrics and will also fade the colours. If the bed receives a great deal of direct sunlight, you would be wise to fold back the quilt or draw the curtains, particularly during the summer. If you have more than one quilt, they can be rotated, thus extending the life of each quilt. This is a good point to remember when your husband or other family member asks why you are making another quilt when you already have a perfectly good one!

Storage

Store your quilt by rolling or folding it and wrapping in an old cotton pillowcase or sheet. If folded, it should be refolded occasionally along different fold lines, to avoid permanent creases. Never store in a plastic bag as air circulation is vital. Do not lie an unwrapped quilt directly on a wooden shelf as chemicals in the timber can produce stains on the fabric.

Washing

If possible, hand wash the quilt in a large container such as the bath. Use warm, not hot, water and dissolve the detergent before adding the quilt. Soak for 5 to 10 minutes then squeeze gently by hand; do not twist or wring. Rinse thoroughly in luke warm water. If you wish to use fabric conditioner make sure it is stirred into the rinse water and not poured directly onto the quilt.

If you have a washing machine which is large enough to take the quilt without having to cram it in, it is a good idea to spin the quilt to remove the excess water as the weight of a water-logged quilt is a strain on the stitching. Use a low speed spin if you have the option on your machine.

Dry the quilt outdoors away from direct sunlight, spread it flat on a clean sheet if you have space, or perhaps drape it over a patio table. If using the clothesline, spread the quilt over several parallel lines rather than hanging the entire weight from one line.

The quilt can be machine washed, especially if you do not have any other container large enough. Do not try to wash a large quilt in a small machine as it will not be cleaned effectively and the lack of space can damage the quilt. However, a large capacity machine which has a gentle cycle can be used, although hand washing is preferable where possible.

Once the quilt is dry it can be placed in a tumble dryer on the air fluff cycle (no heat) to fluff up the batting.

If ironing is necessary, place the quilt right side down on a thick towel and steam press gently from the wrong side.

If you are fortunate enough to own an antique quilt, seek expert advice before doing anything to it. It may be very fragile and it may be better to do nothing rather than risk ruining it.

Finally, it is preferable to keep your pet off the quilt, but if any reader knows of a way to persuade a quilt-loving cat that you did not do all that stitching for his benefit, I would be delighted to hear from you! Fur and fluff can be removed with the upholstery attachment of the vacuum cleaner or the one-way nylon fibre type of clothes brush.

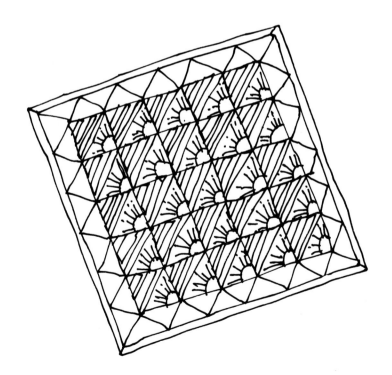

Pieced Blocks

The basis of American traditional patchwork is the pieced block; that is a unit, usually square, which is made up of a number of geometric shapes sewn together. These blocks are then joined, using one of a variety of methods, to form a quilt top. Thus the pattern used to make the pieced block is repeated many times in the finished article, and may form an overall design when joined to other blocks. This is a different technique from the all-over mosaic designs which have generally been more popular in English patchwork.

Often, traditional pieced block designs can be modified so they become suitable for straightforward machine piecing. Many blocks which appear to contain difficult shapes and awkward angles can, if analysed, be made up from simple shapes such as squares, triangles and rectangles. This is done by superimposing a grid over the block design as shown.

(See Fig. 3 a,b,c,d,e,f)

Experimenting with Design

Before cutting into your fabric, equip yourself with some graph paper, tracing paper, coloured pencils or felt tip pens, scissors, pencil and ruler, and spend some time experimenting with patterns. Not only is it fun, but much can be learnt without wasting any fabric. First choose a block design which appeals, from those pictured in

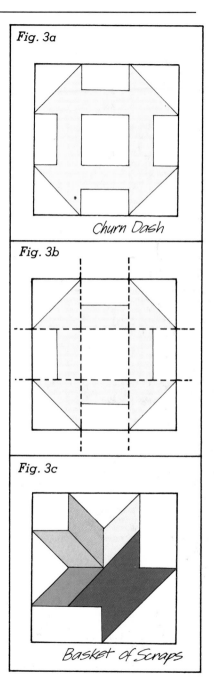

Fig. 3a

Churn Dash

Fig. 3b

Fig. 3c

Basket of Scraps

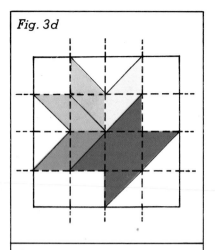

Fig. 3d

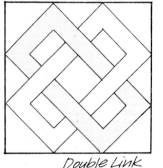

Fig. 3e

Double Link

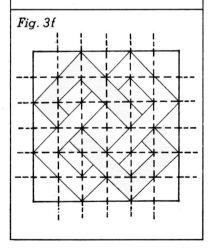

Fig. 3f

this book or elsewhere. Superimpose a grid on the block so you can visualise the basic shapes from which it is composed. Draw the block on graph paper, and colour it in with light, medium and dark tones. Repeat this several times, re-arranging the tones. Observe how the appearance of the block can be substantially altered.

Illustrated is a single block of the Churn Dash design which takes on a totally different appearance with each colour change.

(See Fig. 1 a,b,c,d)

The next step is to consider the effect of joining the blocks together to form an overall design, and the various ways in which they may be joined.

It is important not to choose a design on the basis of the appearance of a single block, because when the blocks are put together they may look quite different. Some blocks form interesting secondary patterns when joined together. In some cases, the secondary pattern may in fact become the dominant design element, depending largely on the colour arrangement.

(See Fig. 2a,b)

In the Shoo Fly block pictured, the brown centre square and triangles form the primary design. However, when six blocks are set together, the gold triangles produce a square which becomes an important part of the design.

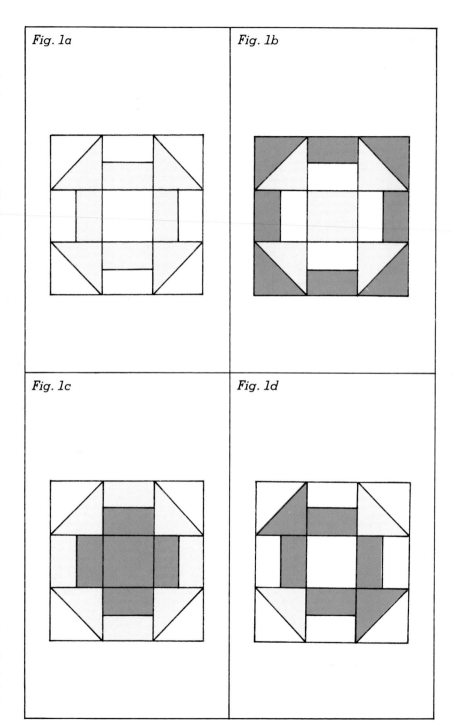

Fig. 1a

Fig. 1b

Fig. 1c

Fig. 1d

Fig. 2a

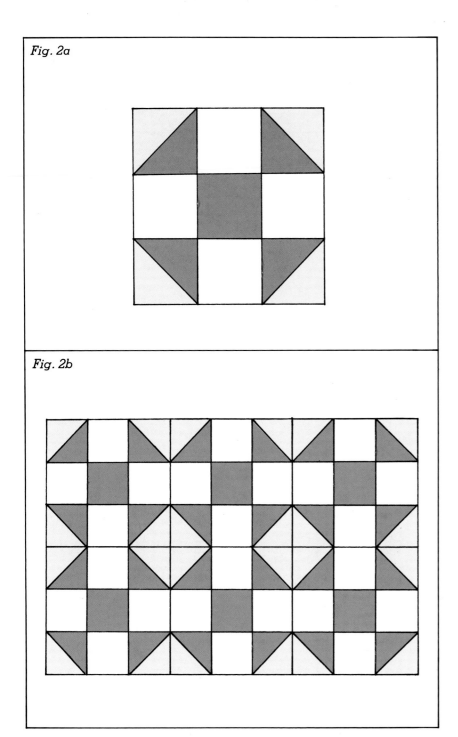

Fig. 2b

Fig. 4

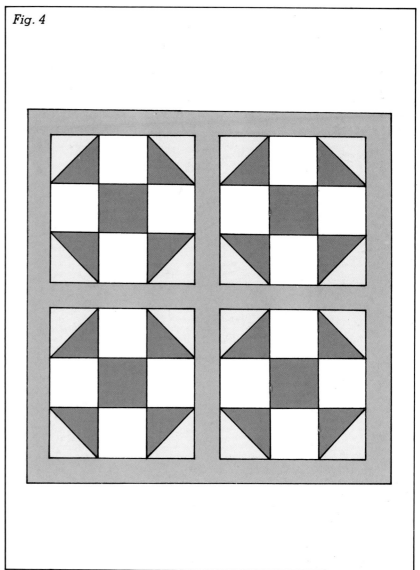

Ways of Joining Blocks

If you wish to preserve the appearance of the single block, you can use dividing strips, called sashing, which frame the block and emphasise its design.

The sashing may be in a contrasting colour, or may use one of the colours from the block. This method has the advantage of increasing the finished size of the quilt without requiring more blocks.

(See Fig. 4)

Fig. 5

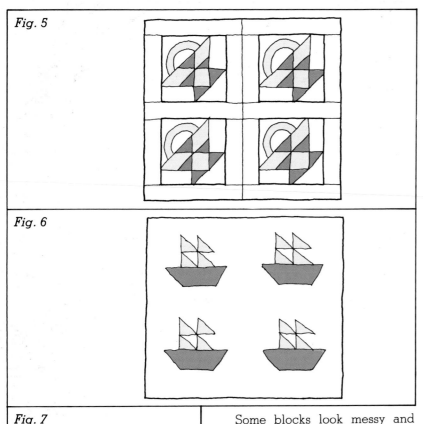

Fig. 6

Fig. 7

Another setting possibility is to alternate the patterned blocks with plain squares. Experiment on paper, because sometimes this technique is marvellously effective, but sometimes it just looks as if you were feeling lazy. Plain blocks demand a fancy quilting design, so this method is ideal for those who enjoy quilting.

(See Fig. 7)

An alternative to the plain block is a secondary block with a simple pattern which combines with the pattern of the first block to produce an all-over design. The famous Irish chain pattern is an example of this.

The primary block contains 25 squares, and the secondary block is plain except for a square appliqued onto each corner. When the two types of block are set together, an intricate design appears, and the two units are no longer apparent.

(See Fig. 7a,b,c)

Some blocks look messy and unattractive when joined edge to edge, so try separating them with a band of the background fabric. Cushions made from a single block also benefit from this treatment because it prevents the design from "disappearing" off the edges of the cushion.

(See Fig. 5)

The dark lines have been drawn to show the block edges. In reality the baskets would appear to float against the background as the boats do.

(See Fig. 6)

Fig. 7a

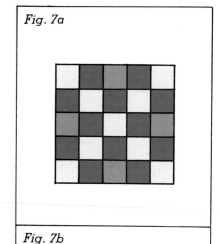

Fig. 7b

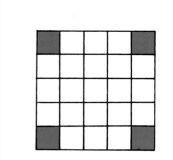

Fig. 7c

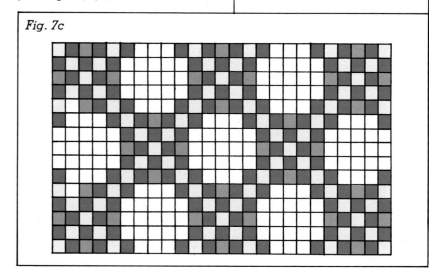

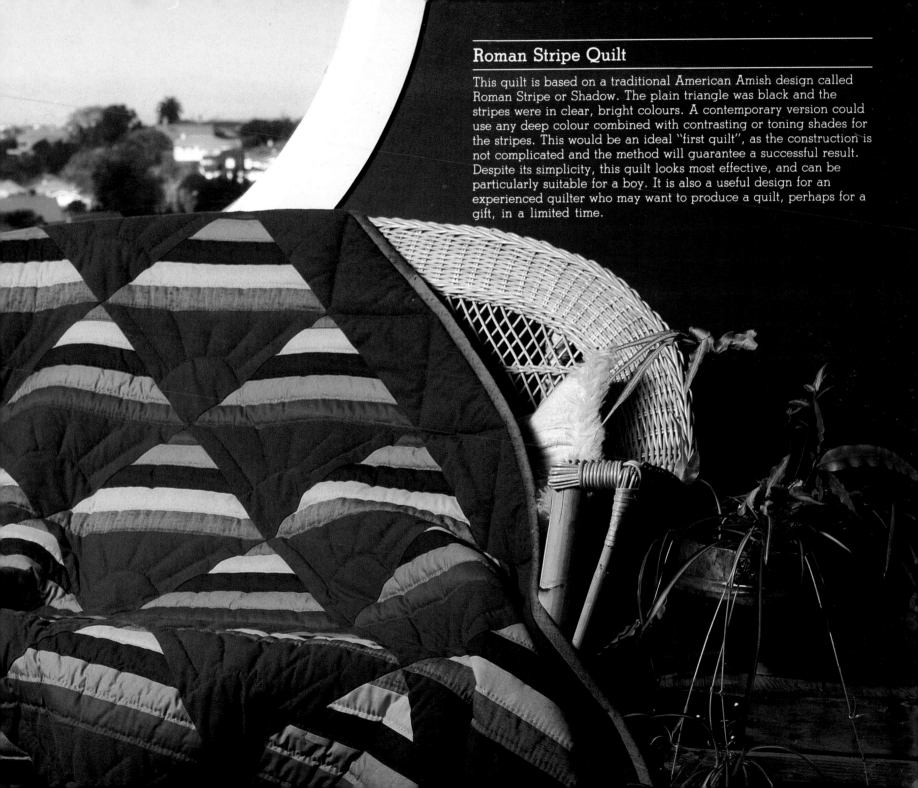

Roman Stripe Quilt

This quilt is based on a traditional American Amish design called Roman Stripe or Shadow. The plain triangle was black and the stripes were in clear, bright colours. A contemporary version could use any deep colour combined with contrasting or toning shades for the stripes. This would be an ideal "first quilt", as the construction is not complicated and the method will guarantee a successful result. Despite its simplicity, this quilt looks most effective, and can be particularly suitable for a boy. It is also a useful design for an experienced quilter who may want to produce a quilt, perhaps for a gift, in a limited time.

Finished Size

60 x 90 inches (150 x 225 centimetres), made up of forty 10 inch (25.5 centimetre) blocks, set 5 x 8 with 5 inch (12.5 centimetre) borders.

Fabric Quantities

Dark fabric for triangles and borders: at least 3¼ yards x 45 inches (3 metres x 115 centimetres) wide. As this amount of fabric is a very tight fit, you could buy an extra ¼ yard (20 centimetres).
¾ yard (70 centimetres) each of five fabrics for stripes.
Binding: 10 yards (9 metres).
Backing: 5½ yards (5 metres) (or a sheet could be used).
Batting: amount required depends on its width.

Cutting

Pre-wash and iron all fabrics.

Cut 10 strips each 2 inches (5 centimetres) wide from each of the stripe fabrics, across the width of the fabric.

Cut two borders 5 x 92 inches (13.5 x 230 centimetres) and two borders 5 x 62 inches (13.5 x 155 centimetres) from the length of the dark fabric. This must be done before cutting any of the triangles.

Make a triangle template 16 x 11½ x 11½ inches (40.5 x 29 x 29 centimetres) from cardboard. (See diagram for dimensions.)

Cut 40 triangles from the dark fabric. See cutting layout. This layout is a very tight fit. If you cannot cut four borders and four triangles from the width of your fabric, you will need to buy extra fabric.

(See Fig. 1,2,3)

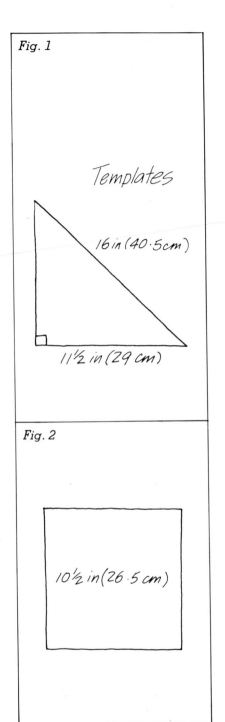

Fig. 1

Templates

16 in (40.5cm)

11½ in (29 cm)

Fig. 2

10½ in (26.5 cm)

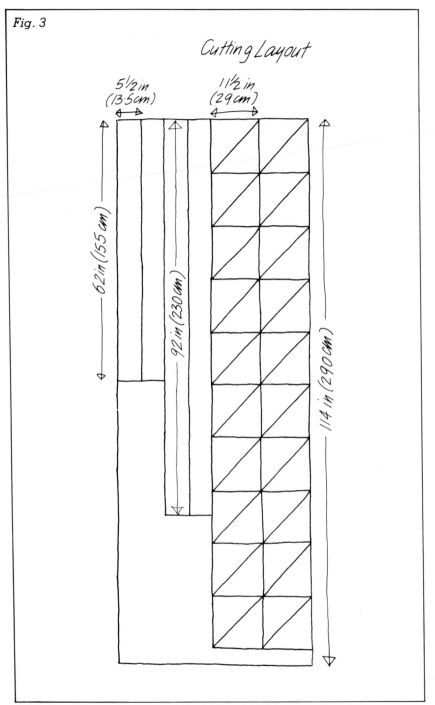

Fig. 3

Cutting Layout

5½ in (13.5cm)

11½ in (29 cm)

62 in (155 cm)

92 in (230cm)

114 in (290cm)

Construction

Allow ¼ inch (6 millimetres) for all seams. Join five strips (one of each colour) to form a band. Make 10 bands. The quilt shown had the strips arranged in the same order in each band, but you may want to vary the order to give a more random effect.

From the wrong side, press all seams to one side. Press again from the right side, making sure there are no folds against the seam line.

Using the triangle template, cut four triangles from each band. Note that the colour at the point of half the triangles forms the base of the rest of the triangles. The seams should be pressed so they face away from the point of the triangle. You will find that half of the triangles will need to have their seams re-pressed so all seam allowances will face away from the side of the seam line where the quilting will be done. This will be much easier without the added bulk of seams.

(See Fig. 4)

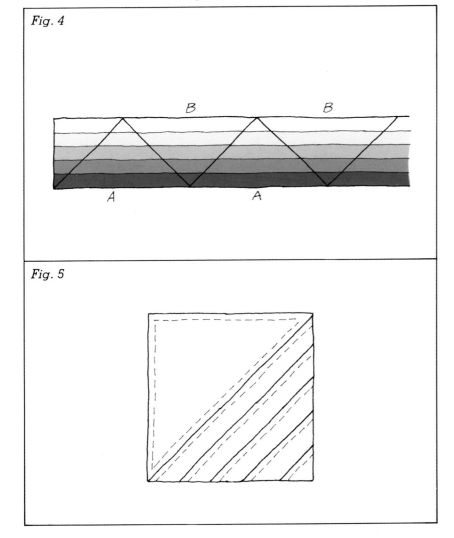

Fig. 4

Fig. 5

Sew a dark triangle to each striped triangle. Have the striped triangle on top, because the seam line of the dark triangle runs along the bias and it is liable to stretch, but the seam line of the striped triangle is on the straight grain and is more stable. Press the seam towards the dark side.

Cut an accurate template 10½ inches (26.5 centimetres) square from cardboard. Place the template over the right side of each square, aligning opposite corners of the template with the diagonal seam line. Trim the excess from around the template, preferably with a rotary cutter, or mark a pencil cutting line and trim with scissors. This may seem to be a waste of fabric but it will produce 40 identical perfect squares which will be much easier to join into a quilt top with all seams matching and each block lying smoothly.

(See Fig. 1,2)

Join five blocks into a row. Have the dark edge on top and the stripes underneath with the seams running away from the presser foot, because this time the dark seam is on the straight grain and the stripe seam runs along the bias. When joining the blocks, alternate the two different types of block, as illustrated above. Press the seams to one side, away from the stripes. Make eight rows. Join the rows in pairs, then join the pairs into two groups of four. Finally join these to form eight rows of five blocks. This method avoids handling as much bulk as you have to if the top were joined row by row. Match the seams carefully as the blocks are joined. Press all seams away from the stripes.

Sew on the borders. Match the centre of each border to the centre of each side. End the stitching, and backstitch ¼ inch (6 millimetres) before the edge of the quilt top. Leave the excess of each border strip free. Have the borders on top as you stitch them on. Mitre the corners (Page 9), trim away the excess, and press.

Assembly

Join the backing, if necessary, and press. Assemble layers and baste securely (Page 10). Cut 10 yards (9 metres) of bias binding 4 inches (10 centimetres) wide (for a double thickness binding). Bind edges (Page 11).

Quilting

The quilting can be done in a number of ways depending on the time available. If you have very little time, or if you want to use thick batting for a puffy and very warm quilt, it would be best to tie rather than quilt.

If you want to do a minimal amount of quilting, simply outline the dark triangle, and quilt along the seam line of the stripes.

(See Fig. 5)

The quilt illustrated has a sunshine motif in the dark triangle. Make a template as shown, using a saucer or similar for the curved edge. Mark lines on it as a guide for marking the rays.

(See Fig. 6)

If you feel inclined, a more elaborate motif could be used.

Anything which fits well into the shape of the triangle would be suitable.

(See Fig. 7)

After quilting, remove the basting threads, and press lightly. Embroider your name or initials and the date on the back of the quilt.

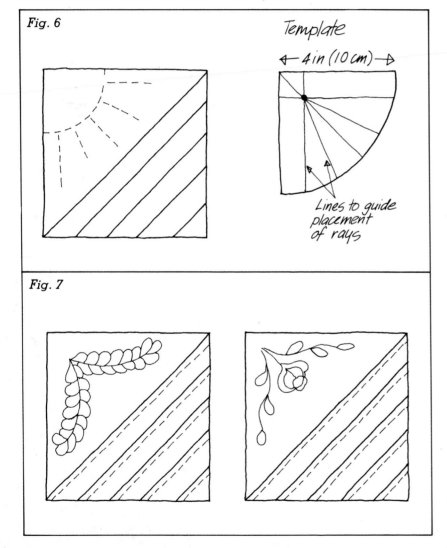

Fig. 6

Template

← 4 in (10 cm) →

Lines to guide placement of rays

Fig. 7

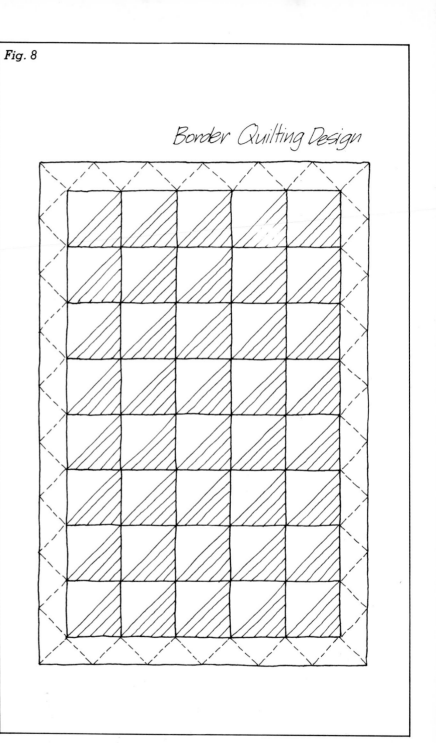

Fig. 8

Border Quilting Design

Eight Point Star

Traditionally, this block is pieced by joining eight diamonds to form the Star, then inserting squares and triangles around the points of the Star to produce a square block. This piecing can be difficult, so for a first attempt, try modifying the block by breaking it down to simple squares and triangles by superimposing a grid (Page 16). Then join the pieces using a logical sewing sequence. This is a very straightforward block which can be pieced in a short time.

Try a cushion first — see how easy it is — then you can make a striking wall quilt using exactly the same method with a few more pieces.

Fig. 1

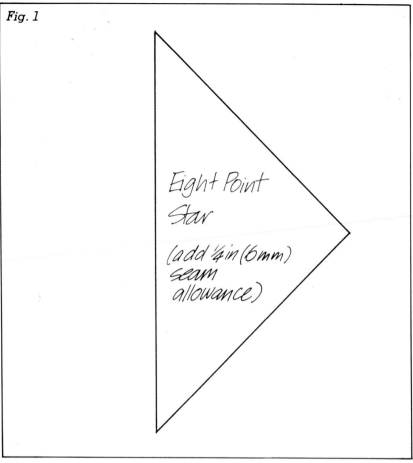

Eight Point
Star

(add ¼in (6mm)
seam
allowance)

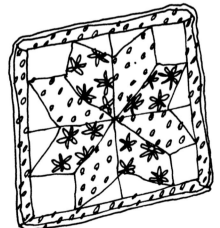

Fig. 2

Template for a 12in (30cm)
Eight Point
Star Block

(add ¼in (6mm)
seam
allowance)

Construction of Cushion

Fabric choice — this method is most successful when the fabrics used are either plain colours or small all-over prints. Avoid large prints or stripes which would require matching at the seam in the middle of each diamond.

(See Fig. 3)

Visualise this block

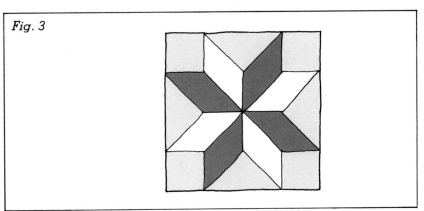

Fig. 3

like this

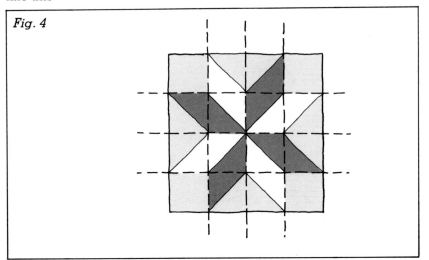

Fig. 4

(See Fig. 4)

From the diagram, you can see that eight triangles of each fabric and four corner squares are required.

Using the patterns given, make templates either by tracing directly onto template plastic and cutting out or tracing onto paper and pasting onto cardboard before cutting out.

Mark and cut the fabric, aligning one straight edge of the template with the grain of the fabric.

Chainsew the triangles together, forming the following units:

(See Fig. 5)

Cut off the points of the seam allowance and press the seams open.

(See Fig. 6)

Lay the units out in the order shown in the diagram and join the units to form rows. Press the seams open. Join the rows, pinning carefully so each seam meets exactly. Press. Cut strips 1½ inches (4 centimetres) wide for the borders. Stitch to each side of the block. Mitre the corners.

Quilt the block if desired, and make up into a cushion, following the instructions on Page 13, 14.

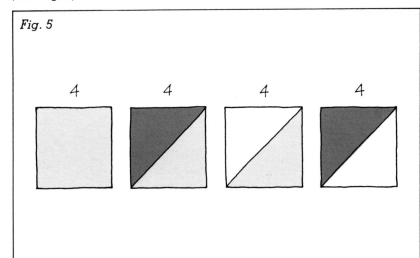

Fig. 5

4   4   4   4

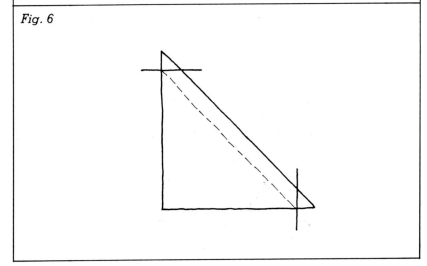

Fig. 6

25

Broken Star Wall Quilt

This striking wall quilt is reminiscent of the traditional Amish work with its iridescent colours and delicate quilting detail.

Fabric Choice

Polished cottons in solid colours have been used to great effect in this quilt. Prints can also be used, but avoid any that need matching at the seam across the diamonds. The instructions refer to the colours in the pictured quilt, but use the colours of your choice.

Finished Size

30 inches (75 centimetres)

Fabric Quantities

Fabric width all 45 inches (115 centimetres)
Pink polished cotton: 20 inches (50 centimetres)
Turquoise polished cotton: 30 inches (75 centimetres)
Black polished cotton: 30 inches (75 centimetres)
Calico for Backing: 32 inches (80 centimetres)
Needlepunch Batting: 32 inches (80 centimetres)

Cutting

Pre-wash and press fabrics. Make templates from patterns given.

From turquoise fabric, cut the borders first. You will need four pieces, 24½ x 2½ inches (63 x 6 centimetres).

You need 32 triangles of each colour, plus 16 black squares. Stack the fabrics with the lightest colour on top and left-hand selvedges together. Pin layers together, and mark 32 triangles on top fabric. Cut through all layers.

(See Fig. 1)

From black fabric, cut 16 squares. Reserve the remaining fabric for binding. From pink fabric, cut 4 corner squares 2½ inches (6 centimetres) square.

Construction

Chainsew the triangles together to produce the units shown beneath. (See Fig. 1.)

Trim off the points from the seam allowances, then press the seams open.

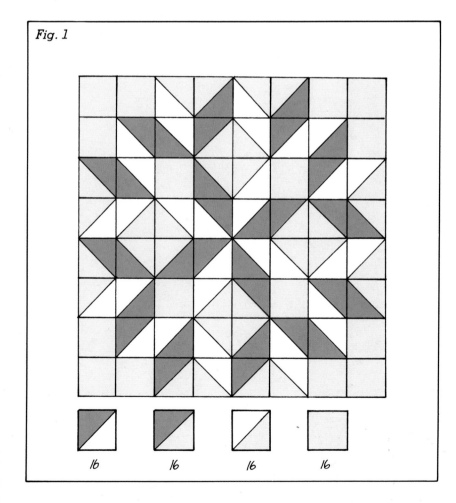

Fig. 1

| 16 | 16 | 16 | 16 |

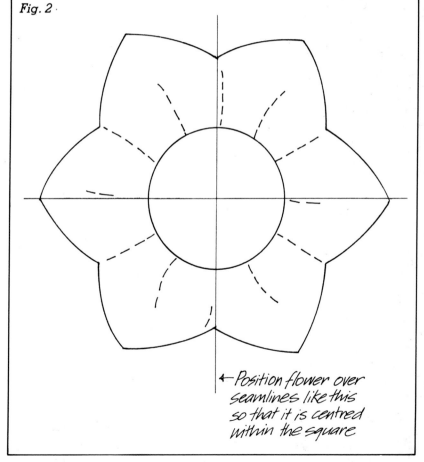

Fig. 2

← Position flower over seamlines like this so that it is centred within the square

Lay the units out according to Fig. 1 and join to form the rows. Press the seams open.

Join the rows, pinning carefully to ensure that all seams meet exactly; unpick and adjust where necessary, because any inaccuracy will be very obvious.

Stitch a turquoise border to the top and bottom edges. Stitch a pink square to each end of the remaining border pieces, then attach to the sides of the Star block, being careful to match the seams at the corners. Press.

Following the instructions on Page 18, assemble and baste the backing, batting and top.

Bind the edges with black fabric (Page 10, 11).

Using a card or clear plastic, make a stencil of the flower design. Use the stencil to mark the solid lines onto the fabric in the large black squares. Draw the dotted lines onto the fabric freehand. A white dressmakers' chalk pencil is the most effective means of marking on black fabric.

(See Fig. 2)

Make a template for the scallop design, and mark it along the borders, as shown. The scallop should coincide with the points of the Star where they meet the border. Connect the scallops with a diagonal line through the corner squares.

Quilt the scallops and flowers as marked. Outline quilt remaining pieces; this will be easier if you stitch just a little more than ¼ inch (6 millimetres) inside the seamlines, so you are not quilting through the extra layer of seam allowance.

(See Fig.3,4)

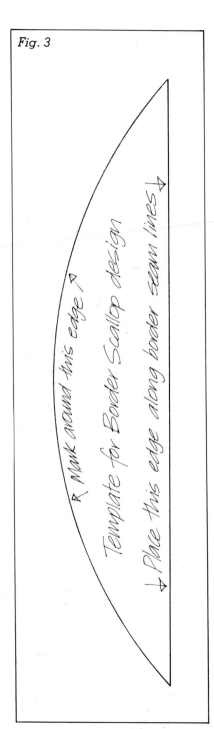

Fig. 3

Mark around this edge

Template for Border Scallop design

Place this edge along border seam lines

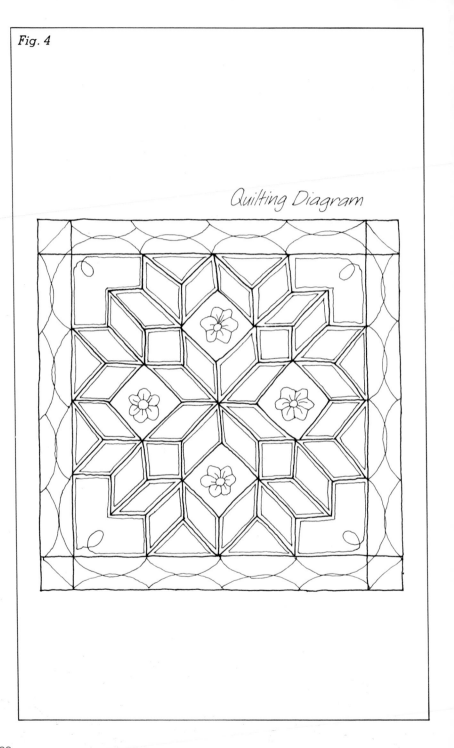

Fig. 4

Quilting Diagram

Dresden Plate

The Dresden Plate design consists of a number of petals joined to form a circle. The petals radiate from a central circle. The outer edge may be finished with scallops or points.

This design combines piecing and applique techniques. The petals are joined by piecing, then the resulting circle is appliqued onto a background square, and the central circle is appliqued over the petals.

Single units of Dresden Plate can be used for many small projects such as bags, cushions or placemats. This design can also be used to make a very attractive quilt which is a realistic undertaking for a beginner, because the piecing is not at all difficult.

Construction

Cut out the required number of petals and the centre circle.

(See Fig. 1)

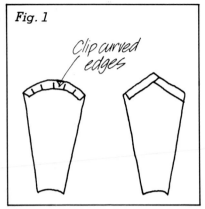

Fig. 1

Clip curved edges

Turn under ¼ inch (6 millimetre) seam allowance on the outer edge, forming scallops or points as desired. Press. Curved edges will need to be clipped.

Turn under the seam allowance of the centre circle.

Try this method for a beautifully circular result: cut a finished sized circle out of card, and cut a larger circle (including ¼ inch (6 millimetre) seam allowance) from the fabric.

Machine or handbaste round the outer edge of the circle inside the seam allowance.

Lay the fabric right side down on the ironing board and place the card circle on it. Pull up the basting thread so the seam allowance is gathered in over the card circle. Press. Remove the card and press again from both sides. This will give you a perfect circle.

Join the petals with straight seams, stitching through the turned under seam allowances.

Press the completed circle, turning all seams in the same direction to one side.

Fold the background square in half, then into quarters. Press lightly, then open out. Using the foldlines as guides, position the Dresden Plate on the square. Pin the outer edges in place, then centre the circle over the inner raw edges of the petals, and pin. Baste the outer and inner edges in place.

(See Fig. 2)

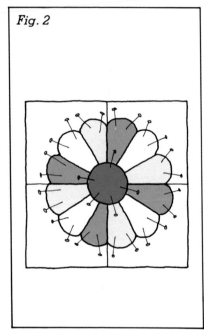

Fig. 2

Handsew to the background square, using either blindstitch or slipstitch. Remove all basting threads, and press.

Templates

Add ¼ inch (6 millimetre) seam allowance when tracing off templates.

(See Fig. 3, 3a)

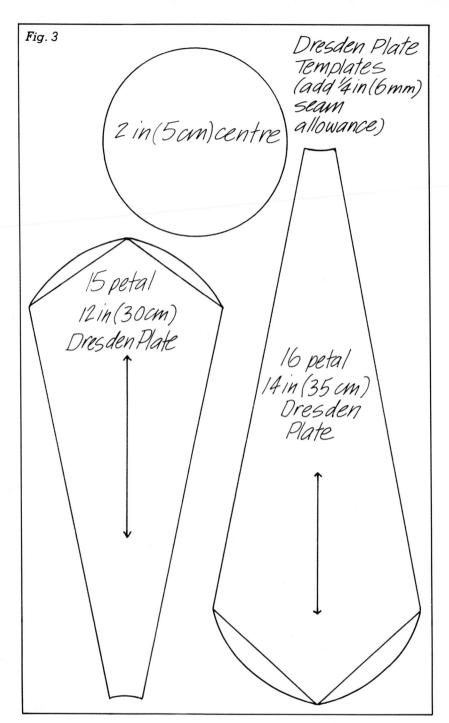

Fig. 3

2 in (5 cm) centre

Dresden Plate Templates (add ¼ in (6 mm) seam allowance)

15 petal 12 in (30 cm) Dresden Plate

16 petal 14 in (35 cm) Dresden Plate

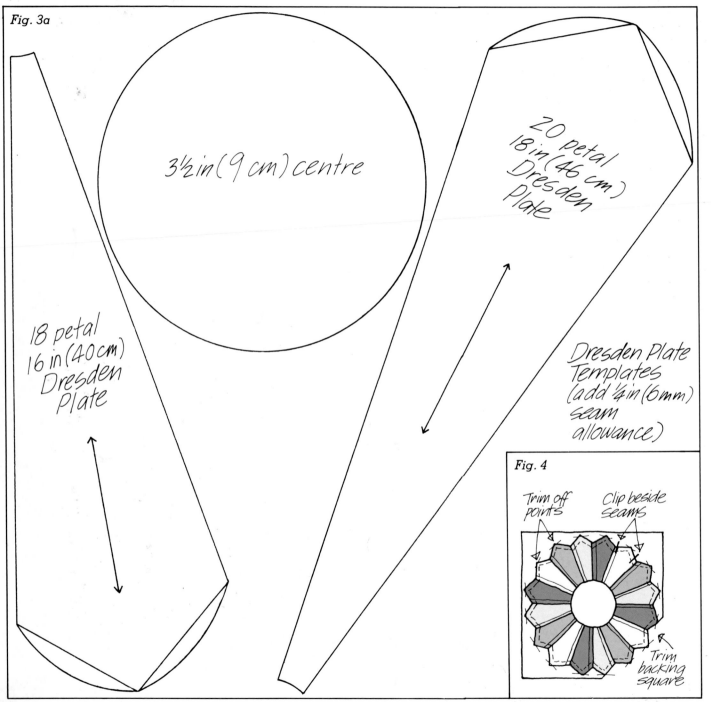

Fig. 3a

3½ in (9 cm) centre

20 petal
18 in (46 cm)
Dresden
Plate

18 petal
16 in (40 cm)
Dresden
Plate

Dresden Plate
Templates
(add ¼ in (6mm)
seam
allowance)

Fig. 4

Trim off
points

Clip beside
seams

Trim
backing
square

Dresden Plate Placemats

Fabric Quantities

Four different fabrics: 10 inches
(25 centimetres) of each.
Backing fabric: 1¼ yards (1.2
metres).

Construction

Pre-wash and press all fabrics.

Make a template from the 16
petal pattern, allowing ¼ inch (6
millimetres) all round for seams.

Cut 24 petals from each fabric
and 6 circles for the centres. Cut
six 16 inch (40 centimetre) squares
from the backing fabric.

Join the petals with straight
seams. Press, turning the seams to
one side.

Turn under the seam allowance
of the centre circles as described
previously. Pin, baste and handsew over the centre of petals.

Lay the Dresden Plate face
down on the right side of a backing square and pin together.
Stitch the two layers together,
pivoting at the points and at the
seams. Have the seam allowances
facing towards you, away from the
presser foot as you sew. Leave an
opening for turning.

Trim the backing square level
with the outer edge of the front.
Trim off the points and clip beside
the seams.

(See Fig. 4)

Turn, and press. Slipstitch the
opening closed.

Drunkard's Path

The variation of possible designs from this block is almost endless. The one shown in the Table Runner is called Fool's Puzzle, but the names are as varied as the designs. The units can be sewn together by machine, but the beginner will probably find it easier to handsew the curves.

Table Runner

Materials

Print fabric: 20 inches (50 centimetres).
Solid colour fabric: 28 inches (70 centimetres). This includes the binding.
Backing: 20 inches (50 centimetres) calico.

Make cardboard or plastic templates of patterns A and B, and trace round these on wrong side of fabric. This will be the sewing line; add ¼ inch (6 millimetres) for seams, and mark notches on all pieces.

(See Fig. 1,2)

Cutting

Cut 16 x A shape print.
Cut 16 x A shape solid colour.

Cut 16 x B shape print.
Cut 16 x B shape solid colour.

Do not cut the binding until all the units have been assembled, then cut two strips 2 inches (5 centimetres) wide the length of the runner plus 4 inches (10 centimetres) and two strips 2 inches (5 centimetres) wide, the width of the runner plus 4 inches (10 centimetres).

It is a good idea to lay out the units on a tray or a large piece of cardboard, one complete block at a time, following the illustration shown. This avoids sewing the wrong two pieces together and having to unpick. Pin each end and the centre of two units, matching the notches. Sew along the marked seam line, easing the fabric round the curve.

(See Fig. 3)

Assemble the units as illustrated; make two complete blocks, and join. Be very careful to match all seams. This is most important. Press.

Cut the calico backing the same size as the runner, and pin the two together. If the runner is to be quilted, insert a light batting between the top and the backing. Quilt ¼ inch (6 millimetres) in from the seam lines.

On the right side, sew on the binding strips using a ¼ inch (6 millimetre) seam; mitre the corners, and slipstitch the binding to the wrong side.

The template can be enlarged or made smaller very easily. Draw a square the required size, place the point of a compass on one corner, and draw a semi circle. Mark notches as shown on pattern.

(See Fig. 4)

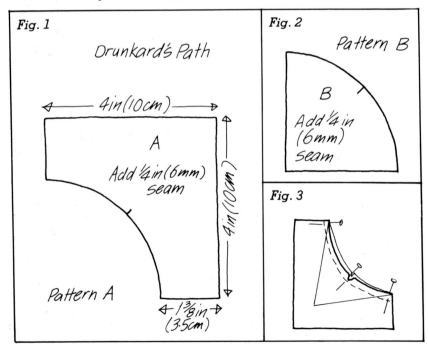

Fig. 1

Drunkard's Path

4in (10cm)

A
Add ¼in (6mm) seam

4in (10cm)

Pattern A

1⅜in (3.5cm)

Fig. 2

Pattern B

B
Add ¼ in (6mm) seam

Fig. 3

Fig. 4

Drunkard's Path Table Runner
Fool's Puzzle

One complete Block

Schoolhouse

Various House designs have featured in American quilt making since about 1870. One of the most popular was the "Little Red Schoolhouse", usually made in red and white. But many other House designs exist.

Wall Hanging

This House block is suitable for machine piecing, and can be used to make a wall hanging.

Pattern

On a sheet of graph paper, draw a 12 inch (32 centimetre) square, and mark the design according to the measurements on the diagram. Cut apart, and paste one piece of each shape onto thin card. Mark ¼ inch (6 millimetre) seam allowance round each piece and cut out the card to produce a template for each shape. Label each template. Or leave the graph paper drawing intact and mark seam allowance around each piece in a contrasting colour, then trace onto clear plastic. Cut templates in plastic.

Cut the following pieces: Front of house — A: two; B: one; D: one. Side of house — C: two; B: three. Roof and chimney — E: one; G: two. Door and windows — A: one; B: two. Border — J: four. Corner squares — K: four.

Join the pieces to form the units shown by the solid lines, then join the units to form upper and lower sections. Finally, join the roof section to the house section. Check that all seams meet accurately, and press. Stitch a border strip J to each side of the block. Stitch a corner square K to each end of the remaining two J, and sew these strips to the top and bottom edges of the block.

(See Fig. 1)

Cut a piece of batting and a piece of backing fabric, each slightly larger than the block, and baste the layers together.

Quilt as desired. Outline-quilt each piece, or quilt the different sections of the house. Details such as clouds, smoke, birds, roof tiles or window shutters could be added. Finish the edges with bias binding, and attach loops to the top edge for the dowel rod.

Jeremy's House Quilt

Having successfully constructed one House block for the wall hanging, you will now have the confidence to embark on a quilt. It requires 24 blocks, joined with lattice strips and framed by a border. Finished size is 68 x 96 inches (172 x 244 centimetres), suitable for a single bed. A larger quilt can be made by adding another border or by increasing the number of blocks.

The quilt illustrated was designed as a scrap quilt to use fabrics left over from dressmaking and other projects. Using the same fabrics for doors and windows and keeping to a colour scheme set by the choice of fabric for the lattice strips gives continuity. If you do not have a wide selection of scraps, or if you prefer a more ordered effect, you may wish to purchase fabrics.

If purchasing fabrics for 24 identical blocks, you will require:
Cream for background: 1 yard (1 metre).
For doors and windows: 24 inches (60 centimetres).
For house fronts: 1 yard (90 centimetres).
For roofs and chimneys: 30 inches (75 centimetres).
For sides of houses: 1 yard (90 centimetres).

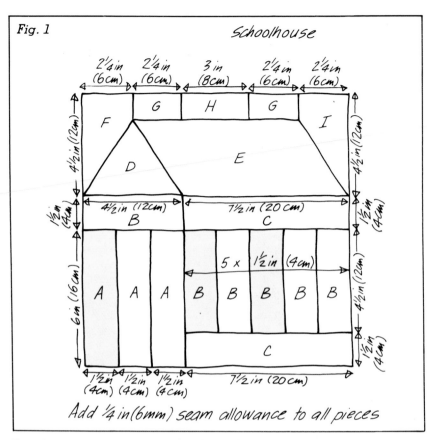

Fig. 1   Schoolhouse

Add ¼ in (6mm) seam allowance to all pieces

For lattices: 1¼ yards (1.20 metres).
For borders: 2¾ yards (2.50 metres).
Backing: a sheet 72 x 100 inches (180 x 250 centimetres) — or 5½ yards (5 metres) of fabric, 36 or 45 inches (90 or 115 centimetres) wide.
Batting: 3½ yards (3.10 metres), 55 inches (150 centimetres) wide (will require piecing).
Binding: 10 yards (9 metres) of double fold bias.

Cutting

J: 58 From the lattice fabric.
K: 30 From the background
F: 24 fabric.

H: 24
I: 24
A: 24 From the door fabric.
B: 48 From the window fabric.
For each block cut from scraps:
From fabric 1 — A: 2; B: 1; D: 1.
From fabric 2 — B: 3; C: 2.
From fabric 3 — E: 1; G: 2.
Borders:
Cut two 72 x 5½ inches (180 x 13.5 centimetres).
Cut two 100 x 5½ inches (250 x 13.5 centimetres).
Binding: Cut 10 yards (9 metres) of double fold bias binding (Page 11).

Block Construction

Follow the instructions given for the wallhanging (page 35), and make 24 blocks. Join five lattice strips alternately with four blocks to form a row. Make six rows.

Join five corner squares alternately with four lattice strips to form a sash. Make seven sashes.

Join the sashes alternately with the rows to construct the quilt top. Press, then sew on the border strips, and mitre the corners (page 8).

Cut the batting and backing, joining if necessary. Assemble the layers (Page 10), and baste. Attach bias binding (Page 11).

Quilting

In each block outline quilt the front, side and roof sections and the door and windows.

Quilt an X in each corner square. Mark the centre of each lattice strip, and rule quilting lines as illustrated. Quilt lattice strips.

(See Fig. 6)

Cut a template for the border quilting design.

Start marking from the mitre seam, with the point of the template extending 1¼ inches (3 centimetres) past the seam.

Mark a row of ovals, starting from each end and meeting in the middle of the border, adjusting slightly in the middle if necessary. Mark a second row of ovals, centred over the meeting point of the first row. Make sure the design is straight and central by marking a line along the centre of the border and aligning the ovals with this line as they are marked.

Quilting this design is simplified by using four needles and stitching four waving lines, rather than trying to stitch the ovals.

(See Fig. 4)

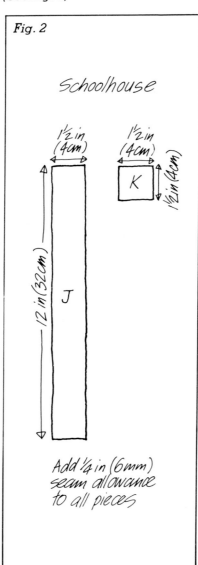

Fig. 2

Schoolhouse

1½ in (4cm)

1½ in (4cm)

1½ in (4cm)

K

12 in (32cm)

J

Add ¼ in (6mm) seam allowance to all pieces

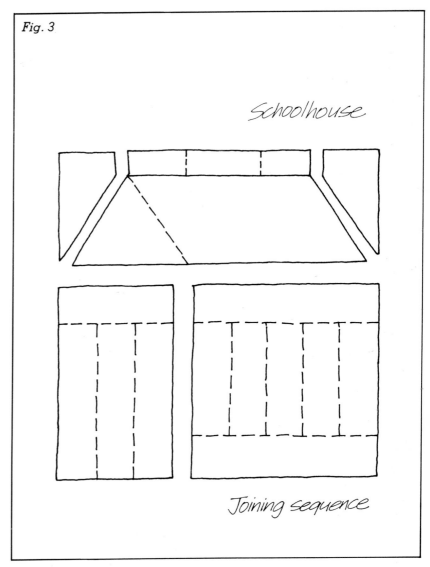

Fig. 3

Schoolhouse

Schoolhouse

Joining sequence

Suggested variations

Personalise the quilt by embroidering names of the family and friends of the child on the door of each house or on the lattice strip beneath the house.

Make a charming quilt for a baby by reducing the blocks to half size (6 inches or 16 centimetres). Keep the lattice strips 1½ inches (4 centimetres) wide, and arrange the blocks four wide by five long. This will produce a finished size of 33 x 40 inches (84 x 104 centimetres) without borders. Enlarge the quilt by adding borders if desired.

Fig. 4

Quilting method – border design

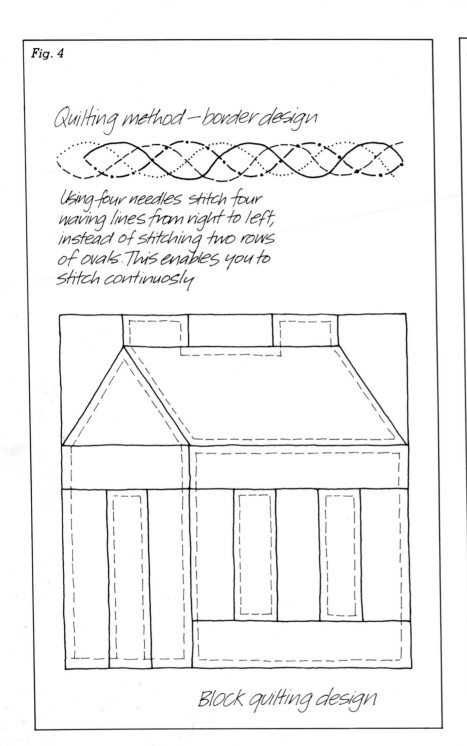

Using four needles stitch four waving lines from right to left, instead of stitching two rows of ovals. This enables you to stitch continuosly

Block quilting design

Fig. 5

Border Quilting Template

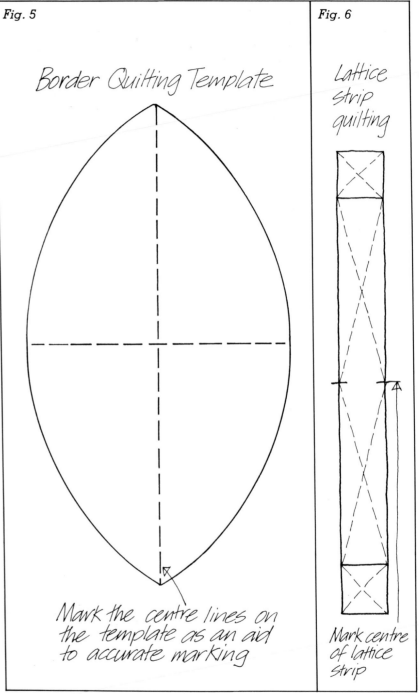

Mark the centre lines on the template as an aid to accurate marking

Fig. 6

Lattice Strip quilting

Mark centre of lattice strip

Log Cabin

Log Cabin is one of the oldest types of patchwork and remains one of the most popular. The design was often used by the early American settlers in the mid-1800s. It was probably favoured because it utilised scraps of fabric too small and too narrow for any other use. Pioneer images are still evoked by this design, with the strips representing the walls of the cabin and a red centre symbolising the chimney, or a yellow central square representing a lighted window.

Colour Choice

The effect of Log Cabin depends on careful choice of fabric colours, either a clear light/dark contrast — dark prints containing shades of red combined with light prints also including red — or two contrasting colours could be used — yellows/greens, for instance.

If you decide to use light/dark contrasts, it is important to distinguish clearly whether a particular print is light or dark. This may be difficult, so try standing back or squinting at the fabric. Usually, the background colour will determine the light/dark quality of a fabric. White, cream or pastel backgrounds usually give the fabric a light appearance. Some fabrics are a genuine medium tone, and are best avoided for this design.

Fabric Quantities

Select fabrics carefully as this, above all, determines the finished effect of your work. If you do not have enough scrap fabrics or if you have a particular colour scheme in mind you may like to buy new material. If you buy ten half-yard (½ metre) pieces of dark tones, ten half-yard (½ metre) pieces of light tones and half a yard (metre) for the centre, you will have sufficient fabric to make 64 blocks, each 8½ inches (22 centimetres) square when finished.

Construction of a Block

Strips of fabric are stitched onto a square piece of backing material, built up around a small centre square. The backing can be calico, cotton or used sheeting.

This layer will not be visible in the finished item.

The size of the backing squares is chosen to suit the size of the project. Twelve inch (30 centimetre) squares are suitable for larger items such as bedcovers; 6 inch (15 centimetre) squares, for cushions or baby quilts. The construction of each square is identical. When enough have been made, they are joined together to form an overall design.

As the same set of squares can be joined in a number of different ways to form a variety of patterns, it is best to make all the blocks for a project before joining any, so they can be laid out in various arrangements before choosing the most pleasing design.

Cutting

Cut the foundation squares ⅝ inch (1.5 centimetres) larger than the desired finished size. Cut the fabrics into strips ⅝ inch (1.5 centimetres) wider than the finished width along the crossways or lengthways grain of the fabric.

Use a template to cut the strips, which should be at least 22 inches (56 centimetres) long and the desired width. You may have a ruler the correct width or a template can be made from cardboard or plastic.

Several layers of fabric can be cut at once. Stack the fabrics with a light coloured fabric on top for ease of marking. Pin the layers together, and mark the strip width on the top fabric with a pencil or fine ballpoint line. Cutting is simplified by the use of an Olfa rotary cutter and cutting mat

(Page 5). Cut the strips into the appropriate lengths for your chosen block size. Cut the required number of centre squares

Assembling

Traditionally strips are sewn in rotation around the centre square. Here, a variation on this method is used: Strips are added to opposite sides of the centre square in each step. This halves the number of times each block needs to be pressed, a worthwhile timesaver when sewing many blocks for a large project, and produces a symmetrical block which uses equal quantities of light and dark fabrics.

Draw a pencil line diagonally from corner to corner of the backing square. Position the centre square so its corners are aligned with the diagonal pencil lines. Stitch in place using a zigzag stitch.

(See Fig. 1)

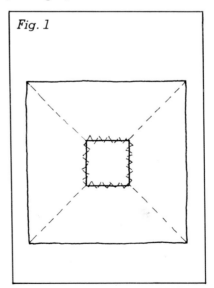

Fig. 1

Place a light coloured strip face down over the centre square, with one long edge even with one edge of the square. Stitch with a ¼ inch (6 millimetre) seam.

(See Fig. 2)

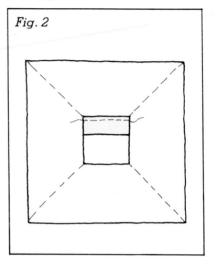

Fig. 2

Place a dark coloured strip even with the opposite edge of the centre square, and stitch it in place.

(See Fig. 3)

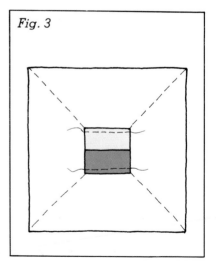

Fig. 3

Fold both strips back, and press. A neat and accurate Log Cabin block requires frequent pressing. This is much less tedious if you can arrange your iron close to your sewing machine so you can use the iron without getting up.

(See Fig. 4)

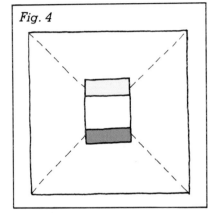

Fig. 4

Place a light coloured strip along the side of the centre square, overlapping the ends of the first two strips. Stitch it in place.

(See Fig. 5)

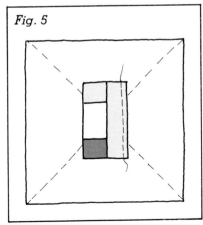

Fig. 5

Stitch a dark coloured strip in

place on the opposite edge. Press both strips back.

(See Fig. 6)

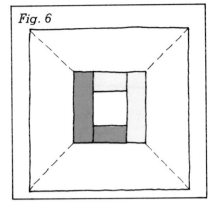

Fig. 6

Continue adding strips in this manner until the foundation square has been covered. Press the finished block, and neaten the edges with a zigzag or overlock stitch.

(See Fig. 7)

Make as many blocks as required for your project, and arrange them in the pattern of your choice. Join the blocks into rows, then join the rows, pinning carefully to make sure the seamlines meet.

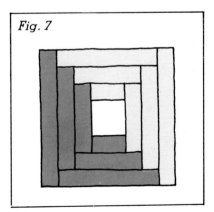

Fig. 7

Log Cabin Quilt

This quilt is suitable for a double bed or larger. It requires 64 blocks, finished size 9½ inches (24 centimetres), which produces a quilt measuring 6 feet 3 inches (1.9 metres) square. Borders can be added to make a queen-size quilt, and the block size can be increased to 12 inches (30 centimetres) to make a king-size quilt measuring 8 feet (2.4 metres) square.

Colour Choice

For a structured colour scheme rather than an all-scrap quilt, you will need four dark prints and four light prints plus a solid colour for the centre square.

For maximum contrast between light and dark when the blocks are joined together, arrange the fabrics so the tones progress from moderately light (or dark) adjacent to the centre square, to lighter (or darker) at the outer edges of the block.

(See Fig. 8)

Rather than choosing all mix and match tiny florals, experiment with different sized florals, stripes, geometric prints and solids. A colour scheme which is too carefully colour-coordinated may produce a rather bland quilt. Try to introduce a touch of something that "clashes", or some variety in the type of print. Choose the fabric for the centre squares last, as an accent.

Fabric Quantities

Fabric A and a: 20 inches (50 centimetres) of each.
Fabric B and b: 32 inches (80 centimetres) of each.
Fabric C and c: 1¾ yards (1.40 metres) of each.
Fabric D and d: 2 yards (1.70 metres) of each.
Centre Squares: 8 inches (20 centimetres).
Foundation Squares: 4¾ yards (4.25 metres).

(See Fig. 9)

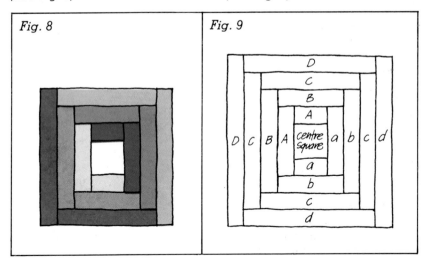

Fig. 8

Fig. 9

Cutting

The cut sizes are as follows (¼ inch or 6 millimetre seam allowance included):
Foundation square: 10 inches (25 centimetres) square
Centre Square: 2 inches (5 centimetres) square
Strip Widths: 1⅜ inches (3.5 centimetres)
Strip Lengths are shown on Fig. 10 (the key to lengths a, A, etc. is shown in Fig. 9).
(See Fig. 10)

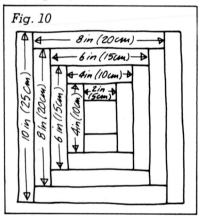

Fig. 10

Cut sufficient fabric for just one block and make it up according to the assembling sequence to check the dimensions and to make sure you are happy with the fabric choice and placement. Then cut 64 foundation squares, 64 centre squares and 64 of each length of strip, i.e. 128 strips of each of the eight fabrics. Make up 64 blocks following the basic method.

Quilt Assembly

The finished blocks may be assembled in many ways. Experiment to find your preference. Some possibilities are illustrated. Once your choice has been made,

join the blocks into eight rows of eight blocks (using a ¼ inch or 6 millimetre seam), then join the eight rows together, matching the seams carefully.

Finishing

Log Cabin which has been constructed using a backing square, has a self-quilted effect and needs no quilting. In any case, the bulk of several layers of fabric would make quilting difficult. This quilt can be simply finished by placing it on a backing sheet (wrong sides together), basting the two layers together, then binding the quilt according to the instructions on Page 10.

Log Cabin Cot Quilt

This quilt is suitable for a cot or as a coverlet on a single bed. It is made up of 48 blocks, finished size 6 inches (15.5 centimetres), which produces a quilt measuring 40 x 52 inches (100 x 130 centimetres), including borders.

Fabrics

This quilt uses a plain/pattern contrast instead of the more usual light/dark contrast. The plain fabrics are in different shades of the same colour — soft pink in the centre, then mid pink and a deep pink at the outer edges.

Fabric Quantities

All fabric 45 inches or 115 centimetres wide. Pale pink, deep pink: 16 inches (40 centimetres) each. Mid pink: 32 inches (80 centimetres). Prints A and B: 12 inches (30 centimetres) each. Print C: 16 inches (40 centimetres).

Centre squares: 8 inches (20 centimetres).
Backing, borders and binding: 2¼ yards (2 metres).
Batting: 54 x 40 inches (130 x 100 centimetres).
Foundation squares, calico or similar: 1⅝ yards (1.50 metres).
Extra fabric in chosen colour for border: 12 inches (30 centimetres).

Cutting Sizes

Measurements in inches (centimetres).
48 foundation squares:
  6½ x 6½ (17 x 17)
48 centre squares:
  2 x 2 (5 x 5)

Print A:
  48 strips 1¼ x 2 (3 x 5)
  48 strips 1¼ x 3½ (3 x 9)
Print B:
  48 strips 1¼ x 3½ (3 x 9)
  48 strips 1¼ x 5 (3 x 13)
Print C:
  48 strips 1¼ x 5 (3 x 13)
  48 strips 1¼ x 6½ (3 x 17)
Pale Pink and Dark Pink:
  12 strips 1¼ x 2 (3 x 5)
  24 strips 1¼ x 3½ (3 x 9)
  24 strips 1¼ x 5 (3 x 13)
  12 strips 1¼ x 6½ (3 x 17)
Mid Pink:
  24 strips 1¼ x 2 (3 x 5)
  48 strips 1¼ x 3½ (3 x 9)
  48 strips 1¼ x 5 (3 x 13)
  24 strips 1¼ x 6½ (3 x 17)

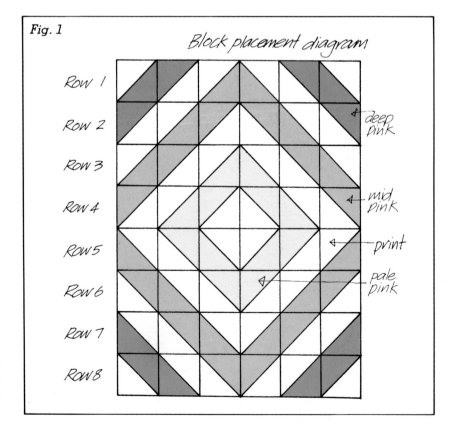

Fig. 1

Block placement diagram

Row 1
Row 2
Row 3
Row 4
Row 5
Row 6
Row 7
Row 8

deep pink
mid pink
print
pale pink

Construction

(See Fig. 1)

Make 48 blocks according to the instructions given earlier.
You will require
- 12 pale pink/print
- 24 mid pink/print
- 12 deep pink/print

Lay the finished blocks out as in Fig. 1. Join the blocks to form rows of six. Join the rows, pinning carefully and matching seam lines.

Cut border strips 2 inches (5 centimetres) wide from your chosen border fabric. (You will have increased the amount of this fabric.) Attach borders, and mitre corners (Page 9).

(See Fig. 2)

Finishing

This quilt could be finished by backing it and binding the edges (Page 11). If you wish to use batting for extra warmth, assemble the quilt as above, and tie it (Page 15).

The quilt shown was tied with pink quilting thread and knotted on the back for an unobtrusive effect, but you could use a decorative yarn and tie it on the front.

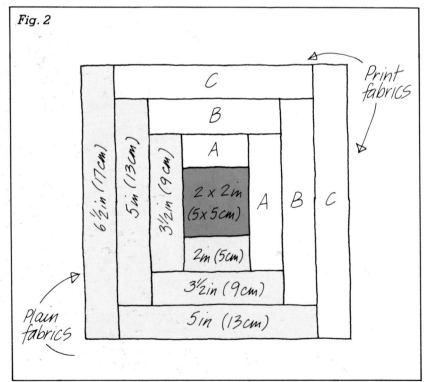

Fig. 2

Print fabrics

Plain fabrics

C
B
A
2 x 2 in (5 x 5 cm)
A B C
6½ in (17 cm)
5 in (13 cm)
3½ in (9 cm)
2 in (5 cm)
3½ in (9 cm)
5 in (13 cm)

Fig. 3

Log Cabin setting variations

a — Barn Raising

e

b — Straight Furrows

f

c — Sunshine Shadow

g — Streak of Lightning

d — Flying Geese

h

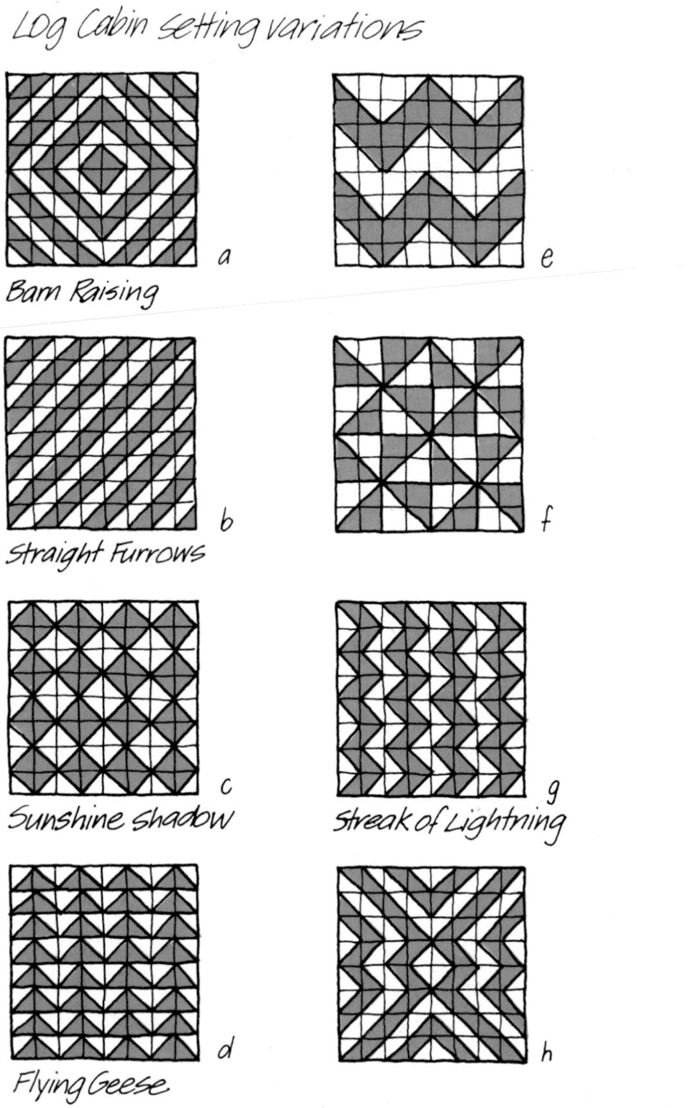

The Log Cabin blocks can be set together to form many different patterns. These designs can all be made from the same 64 blocks. There are many other possible arrangements. Experiment with your blocks before joining them, or sketch a design on paper.

One Shape

Hexagon Patchwork

Hexagon patchwork is a very well known technique. In America it is called English patchwork. A great variety of fascinating optical designs can be created using Hexagon patchwork – flowers, stars, honeycombs – all with the use of this one shape.

The original concept was very simple — to make something useful out of scraps of material. The parts of worn garments which still had some life were not thrown away, but carefully saved to be used again in patchwork.

The hexagon bedspread shown was built up in a somewhat similar manner, although all the materials used were new. Scraps of fabric left over from making dresses, blouses, pyjamas, were all used, provided the material was suitable.

The young owner can point and say, "I remember having a dress made of that material," or her brother can point out his pyjama fabric. It is important to keep the fabrics to a similar weight and make sure they will all wash well together.

The technique is very simple. Two templates are used. The smaller one is the exact size of the patch, and is cut out of a reasonably heavy paper of the type used in large brown paper bags. Open out the bag carefully. Press with a hot iron if the bag is crushed.

Place the paper on a hard surface, and trace round the smaller template very carefully. It is impossible to over-emphasise the need for accuracy. If using scissors, it is a good idea to keep an old pair just for cutting paper, which tends to blunt the edges of scissors. However, if you have an Olfa cutter and mat, it is possible to speed up the job by cutting several layers at a time.

(See Fig. 1,2,3)

The fabric template has a ¼ inch (6 millimetre) seam allowance, but this measurement is not so vital as long as there is sufficient seam left to turn over the paper.

Having cut out a good supply of papers and fabric to start off the project, the next step is to cover the papers. First pin the paper to the wrong side of the fabric.

(See Fig. 4)

Fold over the seam allowance, folding over the corners as you work.

(See Fig. 5)

Start off with a good solid knot, but do not end off the thread so that this tacking thread can be pulled out easily when the papers are removed.

(See Fig. 6)

To join the patches, place the right sides together and overcast the edges with small neat stitches. Use as fine a needle as you can manage.

(See Fig. 7)

Hexagon patchwork can be sewn by the machine, but it is much more suited to handsewing.

The use of a wide variety of materials in the bedspread gives a "confetti" effect, and is a wonderful way of using up all those pieces collected for years. When friends learn of your project, they are likely to be generous in passing on their scraps.

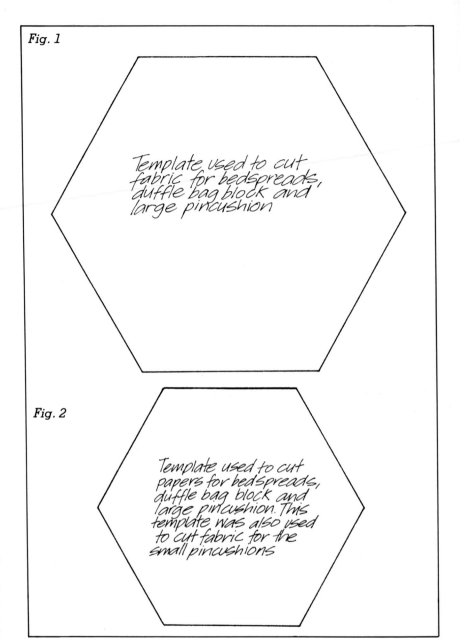

Fig. 1

Template used to cut fabric for bedspreads, duffle bag block and large pincushion

Fig. 2

Template used to cut papers for bedspreads, duffle bag block and large pincushion. This template was also used to cut fabric for the small pincushions

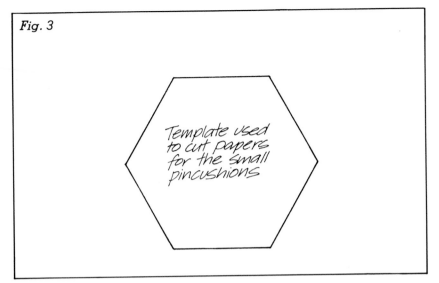

Fig. 3

Template used
to cut papers
for the small
pincushions

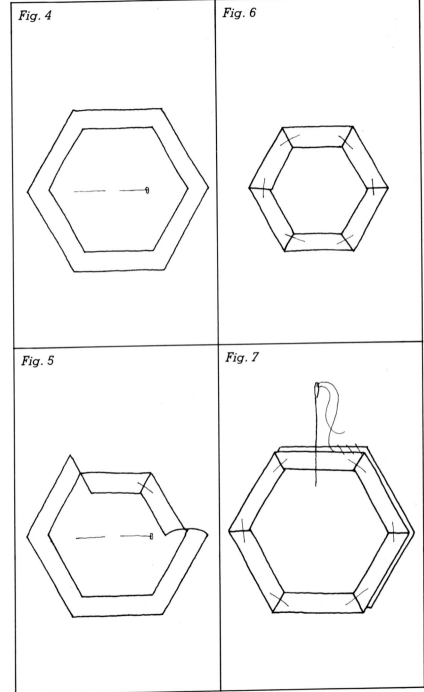

Fig. 4

Fig. 6

Fig. 5

Fig. 7

A single bed sheet was used to back the bedspread, so it was just a case of keeping going until the top was big enough to cover the sheet, leaving a margin of about 6 inches (14 centimetres) all round to finish off the edges.

It is usually convenient to join the patches into blocks of seven hexagons, leaving some single for the final assembly.

Then the time comes to lay all the blocks on the floor to decide their placement.

Having determined the ideal placement, pick up the blocks carefully in rows, and put each row in a plastic bag, numbering each row. Join up the blocks in rows, using the single hexagons that have been kept aside to fill in any gaps.

Press on the right side before removing the papers.

To remove the backing papers, (some of which will have come out of their own accord already) the most simple way is to have someone help you. Spread the

bedspread out over the dining table with the wrong side up, and with a friend at the other end of the table, that chore will be finished in no time at all. Tweezers make it easy to grasp the knot and pull the thread out.

Place the single bed sheet (previously washed and ironed with the hems unpicked) on the floor, right side down. Centre the patchwork with the right side up, on top of it.

Pin from the centre out, radiating to the edges, and then tack very carefully, leaving the edges free. Fold back and pin under the patchwork the border of the sheet extending all round the bedspread.

Hem all round the hexagon shapes, being careful to sew through all three thicknesses to give a good edge to the finished bedspread. Mitre the corners.

Embroider the signature of the maker, that of her helper, and the date on the back of the bedspread.

Small Duffle Bag

Outer fabric: one rectangle 16 x 26 inches (41 x 65 centimetres).
Lining: one rectangle 16 x 26 inches (41 x 65 centimetres).
Lining for pocket: one rectangle 5 x 6 inches (12 x 15 centimetres).
One cardboard circle 7 inches (18 centimetres) diameter.
One 7 inch (18 centimetre) circle of outer fabric, and one of lining for base.
Cord: 2¼ yards (2 metres).
Scraps of fabric for the hexagon flower motif.
Scraps of green fabric for the stems and leaves.
Small amount of fibrefill.

Make two seven-hexagon flower motifs.

(See Fig. 8)

Cut out the stems and leaves from the green scraps, adding a small seam allowance. Press back the seam allowance, and pin the hexagon flower stem and leaves as shown in the photograph; applique in position. From the back, make a small slit in the centre hexagon of each block, pad with a little fibrefill and overcast the slit. Repeat with the leaves. Now, embroider veins on the leaves, and add any other embroidery you may care to do.

Sew the shorter sides together to make a tube.

Sew the pocket to the lining, then sew the shorter sides together to make a tube as for the outer fabric. With right sides facing, stitch the upper edge of the lining to the upper edge of the outer fabric. Turn out to the right side and sew the lower edges of the lining and outer fabric together.

Press the upper edge, and the outer fabric will fold over the lining in the inside. Make a tunnel for the cords by sewing two parallel lines 5½ inches (13 centimetres) apart and 1½ inches (4 centimetres) from the top. Leave a gap in the seam at one side. Cut a slit in the tunnel on the other side and oversew, so the cords can be inserted.

To prepare the base, place the cardboard circle between the lining and the outer fabric, and stitch round. Sew the lower edge of the bag to the base, then zigzag round the seam to neaten.

Cut the cord in two and run each half through either side of the channel and knot it.

Pincushions

For the large pincushion, use the large and medium templates, from scrap material, cut out 14 hexagons from the large template, and from the medium one cut out 14 papers. Construct two seven-hexagon blocks as shown for the bedspread. After the papers have been removed, topsew together, leaving one side open to fill. Stuff with fibrefill, and topsew the opening closed.

The smaller pincushions are made in the same way, but using the medium template for the material and the small one for the papers.

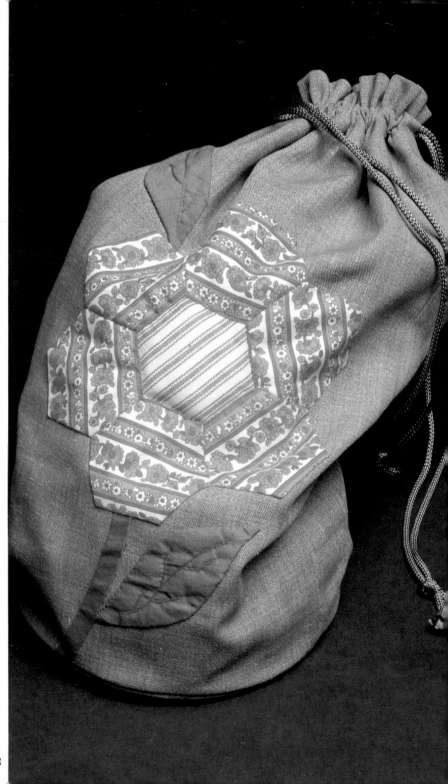

Fig. 8

Small Duffle Bag

Pattern for stems and leaves

Tumbling Blocks

This design, also known as Baby Blocks, is made up of hexagons, each of which contains three diamonds. The shapes used are 60/120 degree diamonds. A pattern is included for two sizes but using isometric graph paper you can easily produce templates in any size required.

The English method of sewing fabric to paper patterns is the best way to assemble Tumbling Blocks; it ensures an accurate result. Two templates are required: one is finished size and is used to cut the papers; the other includes a ¼ inch (6 millimetre) seam allowance, and is used to mark and cut the fabric.

The overall effect is three-dimensional, achieved by using light, medium and dark tones. The tones must be placed the same way in each block.

(See Fig. 1)

Construction

Make two templates, one for papers and one for the fabric, from card or plastic.

Cut papers out. These must be accurate or the patchwork will not fit together. Brown paper such as grocery bags or lightweight card are suitable. It must be firm enough to hold an accurate shape, but not so firm that it is a battle to get a needle through it.

Cut out the fabric. Place the template so two sides are on the straight grain of the fabric.

Pin a paper to the wrong side of a fabric diamond. Turn under the seam allowances and baste over the paper. At the corner, neatly fold the seam allowance over the paper angle, and baste with small stitches to make the angle sharp and accurate. Begin basting from the right side with a knot in the thread, and end with a backstitch, also on the right side. Then when the basting is ready to be removed, the backstitch can be undone and the entire thread pulled out from the knotted end.

(See Fig. 2)

To form the blocks, hold the pieces, right sides together, and join by whipstitching together, then open out the two pieces and set the next piece in place. Be especially careful to join the points securely so there are no holes.

(See Fig. 3)

For a small project, leave the papers in until all the pieces have been joined. Press, then remove the basting threads, and the papers can be lifted out. These papers can be re-used.

If you want the patchwork to have straight edges, cut part shapes to fill in the edges.

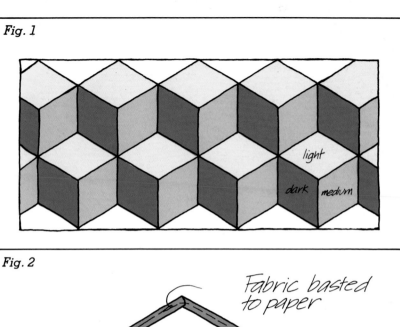

Fig. 1

light

dark   *medium*

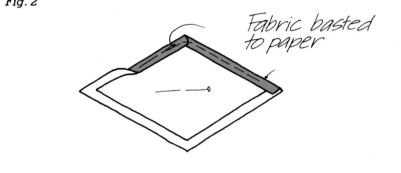

Fig. 2

Fabric basted to paper

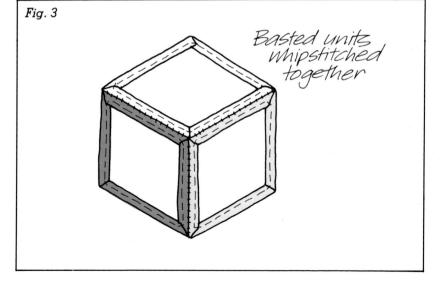

Fig. 3

Basted units whipstitched together

Tumbling Blocks Baby Quilt

Stitch together a rainbow of Tumbling Blocks to make this gaily coloured baby quilt which will double as a nursery wall hanging when outgrown as a cot cover.

Baby Quilt

The panel of Tumbling Blocks is appliqued onto the border strips, and each diamond is outline quilted. The quilt has a different colour for each row of blocks, representing the colours of the rainbow. You could, however, use the same fabrics for every row.

The finished size is 32 x 26 inches (80 x 66 centimetres).

(See Fig. 1,2)

Fabric Quantities

Backing fabric: 36 x 28 inches (90 x 70 centimetres).
Batting: 36 x 28 inches (90 x 70 centimetres).

Bias binding: 2 inches (5 centimetres) wide, 4 yards (3.5 metres).
Small quantities of a variety of fabrics for the blocks and borders.

Light, medium and dark tones of each of the following colours: red, orange, yellow, green, blue, indigo and violet — a total of 21 different fabrics. You will require a 6 x 18 inch (15 x 45 centimetre) piece of each fabric.
Background strips: 8 inches (20 centimetres).
Inner borders: 8 inches (20 centimetres).
Outer borders: 10 inches (25 centimetres).

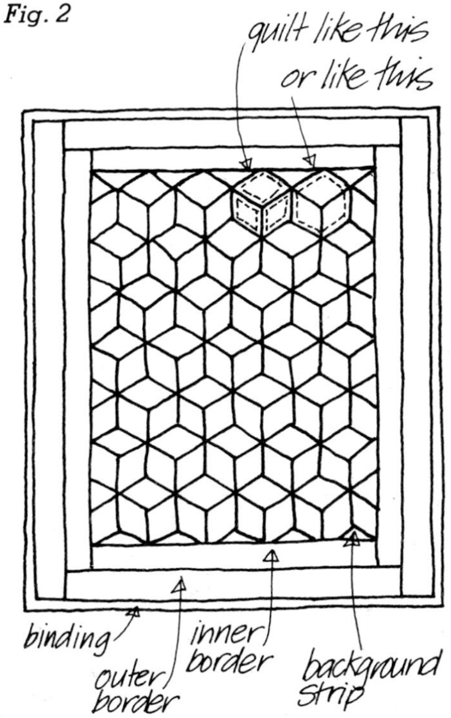

Templates

Use the 4½ inch (11 centimetre) templates and the partial shape templates. Trace off and make templates from card or clear plastic.

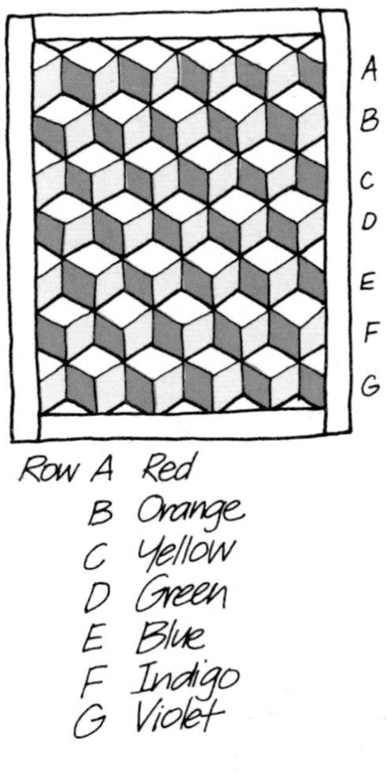

(See Fig. 4)

Method of Construction

Cut 101 diamond papers and eight half diamond papers.

Cut five fabric diamonds from each dark fabric and five from each medium fabric. From the light fabrics, cut either five or four plus two half diamonds. See diagram.

Baste the fabrics to the papers (Page 51).

Join the light, medium and dark diamonds to form hexagons. Join the hexagons to form rows of each colour. Join the rows to form the panel of Tumbling Blocks.

Press, then remove the basting threads and lift out the papers. Press again, making sure that the seam allowances around all four sides are pressed under.

Cut a background strip 1 inch (2.5 centimetres) wider than the panel of blocks and 4 inches (10 centimetres) deep. Press under the raw edges at each end and along the top edge. Place under the top row of blocks so the upper points of the blocks are level with the upper edge of the background strip. Pin and baste in place.

Blindstitch the upper edge of the blocks to the background strip. Trim excess background strip from under the Tumbling Blocks.

Repeat for the lower edge.

Cut border strips 1¾ inches (4.5 centimetres) wide, and applique the

panel of Tumbling Blocks to the border strips.

Cut outer border strips 2¼ inches (5.5 centimetres) wide, and stitch to top and bottom edges, then to side edges. These can be machine stitched. Assemble and baste the three layers (Page 10). Bind the edges (Page 10).

Outline quilt each diamond, or if you have little time available, just quilt each hexagon.

(See Fig. 2)

If this is a gift for a new baby, you may like to embroider the name and date of birth in the top or bottom border.

(See Fig. 3)

It is interesting to note in the diagram above how a "Star and Block" pattern is formed simply by altering the colour placement of the diamonds.

Fig. 1

Row A Red
    B Orange
    C Yellow
    D Green
    E Blue
    F Indigo
    G Violet

Fig. 2

quilt like this or like this

binding
outer border
inner border
background strip

Fig. 4

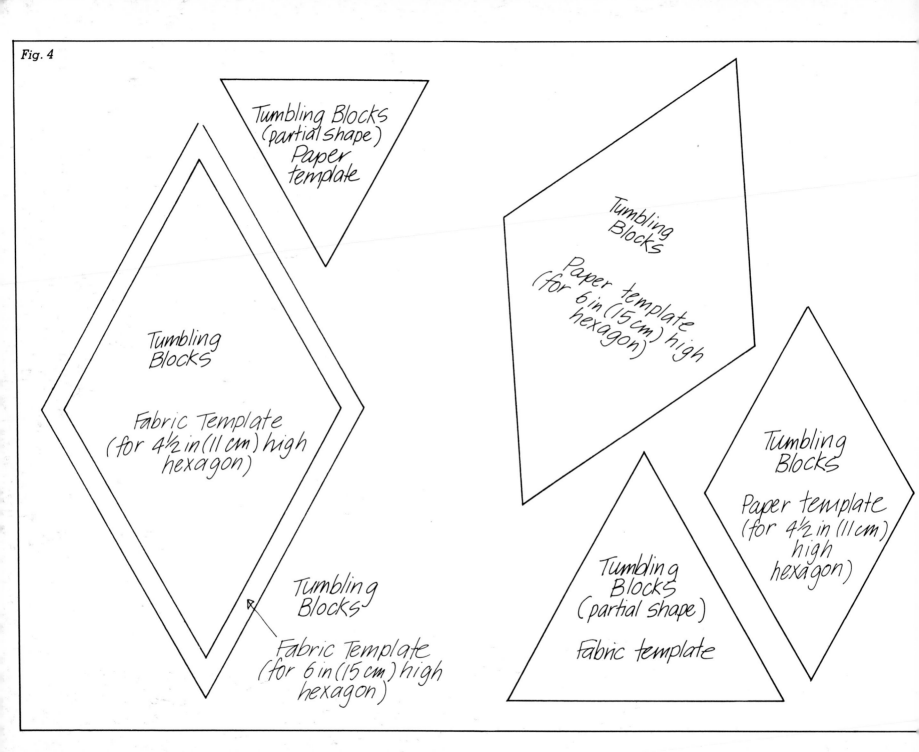

Tumbling Blocks (partial shape) Paper template

Tumbling Blocks Fabric Template (for 4½ in (11 cm) high hexagon)

Tumbling Blocks Fabric Template (for 6 in (15 cm) high hexagon)

Tumbling Blocks Paper template (for 6 in (15 cm) high hexagon)

Tumbling Blocks Paper template (for 4½ in (11 cm) high hexagon)

Tumbling Blocks (partial shape) Fabric template

Clamshell

The Clamshell shape is made up of a semicircle and two quarter circles. Two pattern pieces are required. The larger one for cutting out the fabric includes a 6 millimetre seam allowance, while the smaller one is the exact size of the finished shell. Remember when cutting the fabric that this shape tends to look best in a fairly formal repetition of the pattern such as the diagonal stripe effect used in the tea-cosy.

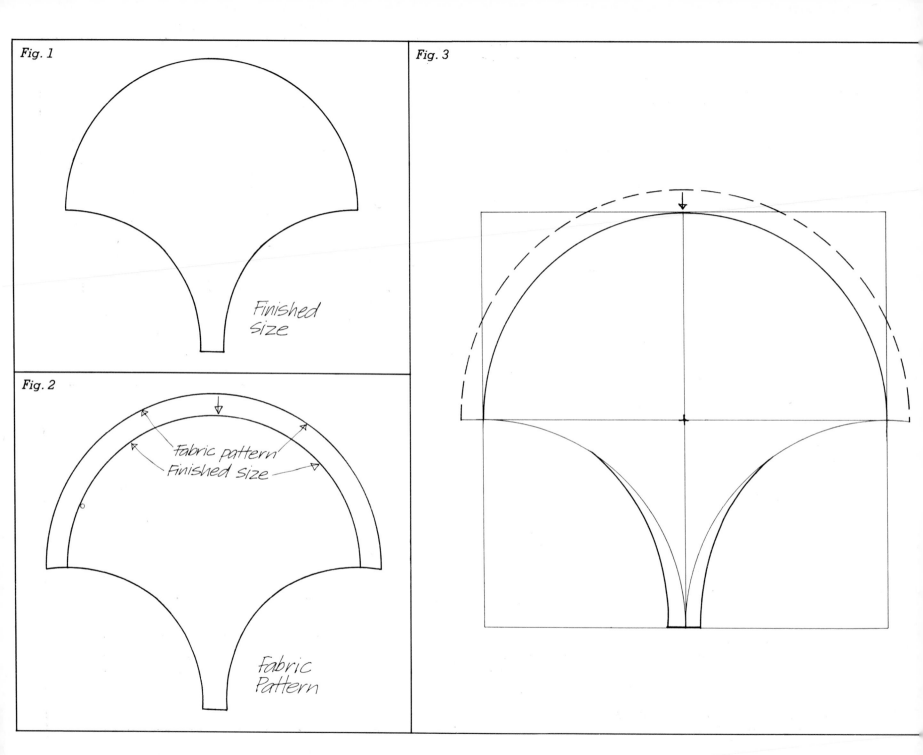

Fig. 1

Finished
Size

Fig. 2

Fabric pattern
Finished size

Fabric
Pattern

Fig. 3

Make templates by tracing patterns A and B onto cardboard or plastic. (See Figs. 1, 2 and 3.)

If a different sized shell is required, draw a square the height and width of the desired sized shell. Find the centre of the square. Pivot the point of a compass on the centre, extend the pencil leg along the horizontal centre line to the side of the square, then form a semi-circle in the upper half of the square. With the compass at the same setting, place the pivot at the lower left hand corner and form a quarter circle. Repeat at the right hand corner. Do not forget to add a ¼ inch (6 millimetre) seam allowance to the new template.

Cushion

The clamshell design can look very effective when plain colours are used and arranged to form diagonal bands of each colour.

You can form the shell shapes by machine basting round the curved edge of each shell within the seam allowance. Place the shell face down on the template over it and pin in place. Draw up the machine basting thread so the seam allowance is gathered in, and press. This method produces a very smooth curve.

Cut the required number of shells of each colour.

Cut all shells full size, even though some of the edge shells will be trimmed by half when the borders are attached. Lay the shells on the backing fabric, starting with the top row. Choose a backing fabric in a toning colour and allow it to show between the shells in the top row, or baste a

piece of fabric in place between the shells in a matching colour. Pin and baste each row of shells in place then blindstitch neatly with matching thread.

On the right side, mark a line ¼ inch (6 millimetres) outside the finished edge, and trim off the excess shells and backing fabric. Attach border strips using a ¼ inch (6 millimetre) seam. Mitre the corners. Make up into a cushion (Page 13, 14).

Tea Cosy

Measurements: 11½ x 9 inches (29.5 x 24 centimetres).

Material Quantities

Five fabrics for the shells: 10 inches (25 centimetres) of each.
Calico for backing and lining: four rectangles 12 x 10 inches (30 x 25 centimetres).
Batting: 10 inches (25 centimetres).
Bias binding: 28 inches (70 centimetres).

Cutting

Outer fabric. Refer to the photograph and Fig. 4, for suggested placement of patches. Cut out the required number of shells for both sides in each of the outer fabrics. Where only part shells are used around the edge, it will be necessary to cut off the surplus.

(See Fig. 4)

Cut the lining, batting and the backing to the required shape. (Page 56).

(See Fig. 5)

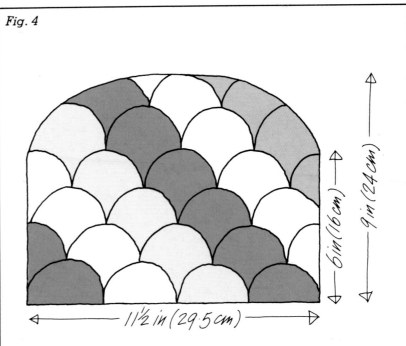

Fig. 4

6 in (16 cm)
9 in (24 cm)
11½ in (29.5 cm)

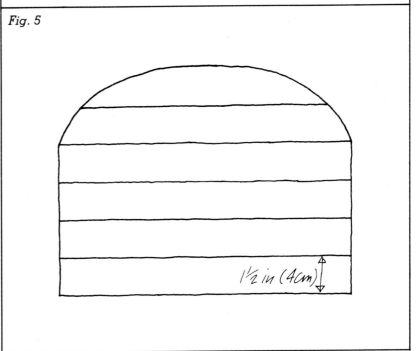

Fig. 5

1½ in (4 cm)

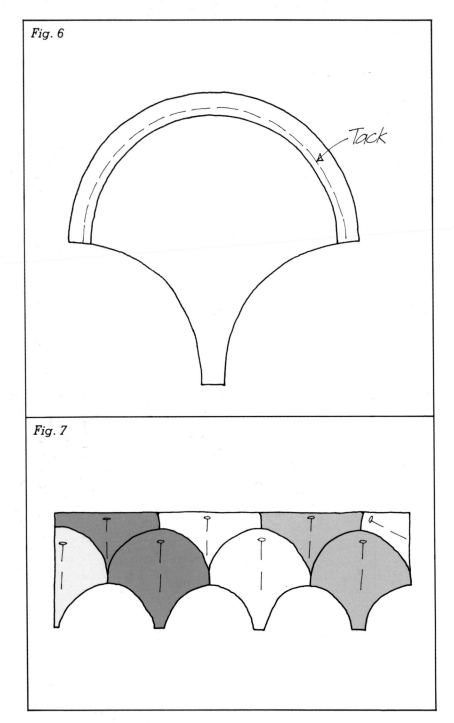

Fig. 6

Tack

A

Fig. 7

On the two backing pieces, mark with a pencil, or preferably, press in with a hot iron, six lines 1½ inches (4 centimetres) apart; press in a vertical line down the centre. Pressing in the guide lines means that these can be seen from the back as well as the front.

(See Fig. 5)

To prepare the shells, trace round pattern B on the fabric, remembering to mark the centre at the top as shown on the pattern. This line is the cutting line. Place pattern A on the right side of the fabric, and trace round the top edge only, as in Fig. 6. Press seam allowance to the back and tack.

An alternative method of preparing the shells is to cut three or four pattern A out of light cardboard. Now, instead of tacking the seam allowance, lay the fabric piece on the ironing board, right side down. Put one of the light cardboard patterns on top of the fabric. Draw the curved edge tautly over the card, and press it down firmly with a hot iron. The process is made easier if the fabric is dampened first. You will find the fabric has to be tucked together in three or four places to make it lie flat. Remove the card,

and give the patch a final press. When the card begins to lose its shape, discard it and use another one. If some of the fabrics seem to be a little too springy to crease well, try a little spray-on starch instead of damping with water.

Having prepared all the patches, lay them down and move them round until you are happy with their arrangement. Starting at the top, put the first row of shells in a straight line putting the middle one in first. (Use the pressed-in lines as a guide.) Pin each one in place and then position the part shells in the gaps. Sew these as neatly and unobtrusively as possible. Continue in the same way until one side of the cosy is covered with shells. Repeat on the second side of the cosy.

(See Fig. 7)

To assemble the cosy, place the lining right side down, then the batting, and then the Clamshell piece on top, right side up. Oversew the three layers together, then repeat with the second side.

Bind the bottom edges of both sides of the cosy. Pin the two halves together, and tack round the perimeter. Bind the raw edge.

Other Shapes

Stripwork

Stripwork is a very useful technique, especially for utility items because it uses a speedy quilt-as-you-go machine method which is durable and easily washed.

It is particularly suitable for placemats, bags, clothing and small purses.

The construction method pieces the top layer, and quilts all three layers simultaneously. An added advantage is that the finished article is reversible.

Cosmetic Purse

Choice of Fabric

A wide range of fabrics are suitable for this technique. Cottons and blends are easy to handle, and they wash well, but heavyweight fabrics can also be used because they can be sewn successfully on the machine and are strong enough to withstand the wear which bags and clothing are likely to receive.

Needlepunch batting is recommended as it is firm and flat, but you may use polyester batting if you prefer. For clothing it is probably more suitable.

Cut a rectangle 8½ x 13½ inches (22 x 34 centimetres) from batting, and another the same size from backing fabric.

Place the backing fabric right side up on the batting. Pin, then baste diagonally and around the edges. This is important because without pinning and basting the bottom layer will be wrinkled as the strips are sewn in place.

(See Fig. 1)

Cut seven strips of different fabrics, each 1½ x 13½ inches (4 x 34 centimetres). Stripwork is more pleasing if you choose fabrics that blend rather than contrast — quite the opposite principle to other types of patchwork.

Place the first strip face up along the left hand edge of the batting. Place the second strip face down on top of the first. Pin, then stitch through all thicknesses — two strips, the batting and the backing.

Turn the second strip so it is face up, and press lightly. Lay the third strip face down on the second, and stitch. Repeat this procedure until all the strips have been sewn in place.

(See Fig. 2)

Sew bias binding to one short edge, turn to the wrong side and slipstitch in place. Homemade bias binding is much cheaper and better quality than bought binding (Page 10). Fold the rectangle as shown, and baste the edges together. Trim the upper corners to give a curved edge.

(See Fig. 3)

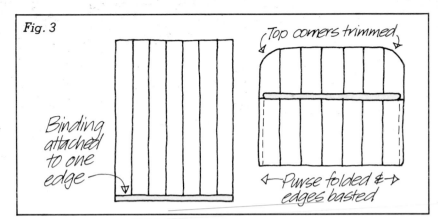

Fig. 3

Binding attached to one edge →

Top corners trimmed

← Purse folded & → edges basted

With the back of the purse facing you, attach bias binding, beginning at lower edge, continuing across the top, then down the other side. Trim seam to ⅛ inch (3 millimetres), turn bias to the other side and slipstitch in place.

Turn the flap down, and press lightly. Apply a press stud fastening or if you prefer, a Velcro self adhesive Handy Dot or a button and buttonhole.

This basic purse can be varied to suit your needs. The size of the rectangle can be altered to make a purse of any size, and the number and width of the strips changed to suit.

(See Fig.4)

Variations

Line the purse with pure silk to make a pouch to protect and maintain the lustre of a string of pearls.

Attach a length of binding to make a shoulder or neck strap for a little girl's purse.

Use plain colours in bold shades instead of prints.

Apply the strips diagonally or chevron-style.

A large carryall bag can be made from a large rectangle of stripwork with webbing handles stitched on. The rectangle is stitched to oval gussets of stripwork, and a zip is inserted in the top opening.

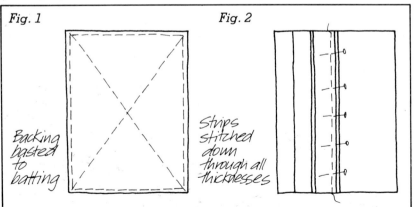

Fig. 1

Backing basted to batting

Fig. 2

Strips stitched down through all thicknesses

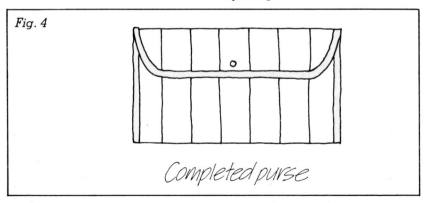

Fig. 4

Completed purse

Stripwork Placemats

These attractive placemats are very practical, as the batting protects the table top. They are reversible, so can give variety with a different colour on the other side.

Fabric Quantities

For six mats:

Backing fabric: 45 inches (115 centimetres) wide, 1¼ yards (1.2 metres).

Needlepunch batting: 1¼ yards (1.2 metres).

Varying quantities of fabric for the strips, depending on how many different fabrics are used. About 10 inches (25 centimetres) of six or more fabrics.

Bias binding cut 1¾ inches (4 centimetres) wide: 7¾ yards (7 metres).

Construction

Cut a 12 x 16 inch (30 x 40 centimetre) rectangle from sturdy cardboard. Using a saucer or similar, draw a curve across each corner and cut to this shape. This will give you a template for oval mats as pictured, but you can make the mats any shape and size you want.

(See Fig. 1)

Use the template to cut six ovals from the backing fabric, and six batting ovals. Baste the backing fabric to the batting, right side up. Do not skip this step if you want reversible mats. Apply the strips diagonally in the same manner used to make the purse. Leave enough excess at the top of each strip for it to cover the batting when pressed forward.

Cut the strips 1½ inches (4 centimetres) wide across the full width of the fabric. Do not cut to length until after the strip has been attached.

When all the strips have been sewn in place, press lightly and trim off any excess from the strips.

(See Fig. 2,3)

Choose fabric for the bias binding which tones with the strips and also with the backing fabric. With the strip side facing, attach the bias binding. Stretch it very slightly as you sew, but not too much or the mats will not lie flat.

Trim seam to ⅛ inch (3 millimetres); turn bias binding to other side, and slipstitch in place.

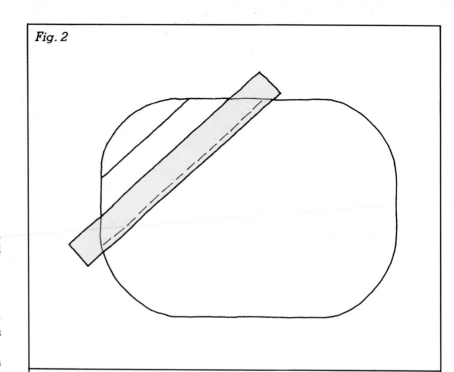

Fig. 2

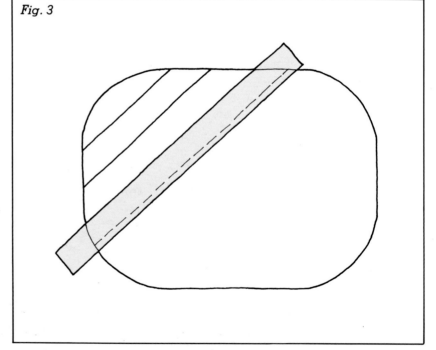

Fig. 3

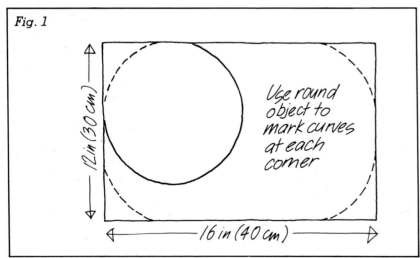

Fig. 1

12 in (30 cm)

16 in (40 cm)

Use round object to mark curves at each corner

Cathedral Window

The Cathedral Window square is traditionally made from
unbleached calico and scraps of printed fabric, but today a
variety of fabrics is used.

The Cathedral Window square consists of two squares of fabric — the Window fabric, usually unbleached calico or a solid fabric and the Window patch fabric of print or contrasting colour. The solid and print fabrics may be interchanged, but the petal design shows up more effectively when a solid fabric is used for the Window. A layer of batting placed under the Window patch (cut ¼ inch or 6 millimetres smaller than the fabric) gives an added dimension, but is optional.

All fabric quantities are based on 45 inch (115 centimetre) width. Wash all fabrics first.

The importance of absolute accuracy in cutting and sewing cannot be over-emphasised. This is the only way to achieve a good finish.

The chart below will be helpful when assessing the size of square and the amount of fabric required for the planned project.

Cutting

Make cardboard templates of required sizes for Windows and Window patches. Draw round the templates on the wrong side of the fabric. This is the cutting line. Do not cut more than two squares at a time, unless you are using a rotary cutter, as the squares tend to become uneven when cutting too many layers. Window squares must be cut on the straight grain of the fabric, but this is not necessary for the window patches.

Preparing the Window

Fold window squares in half, right sides together. Stitch across the ends with ¼ inch (6 millimetre) seam. Sew the window by hand or machine.

(See Fig. 1)

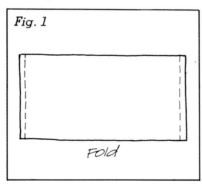

Fig. 1

Fold

Window Square SIZE	Final Window SIZE	1 Yard (1 Metre) Fabric YIELDS	Window Patch SIZE
18 ins (46 cm)	8½ ins (22 cm)	4	5 ins (13 cm)
11 ins (28 cm)	5 ins (13 cm)	12	3 ins (7.6 cm)
10 ins (25 cm)	4¾ ins (12 cm)	12	2¾ ins (7.0 cm)
9 ins (23 cm)	4 ins (10 cm)	20	2½ ins (6.4 cm)
8 ins (20 cm)	3¾ ins (9.5 cm)	20	2¼ ins (5.7 cm)
7 ins (18 cm)	3¼ ins (8.3 cm)	30	2 ins (5.1 cm)
6 ins (15 cm)	2¾ ins (7.0 cm)	42	1½ ins (3.8 cm)
5 ins (13 cm)	2¼ ins (5.7 cm)	63	1¼ ins (3.2 cm)

Open the rectangle and pin seams together at centre so they will not shift when sewing the next seam. Take a ¼ inch (6 millimetre) seam stitch across, leaving a 1½ inch (4 centimetre) opening in the middle. Trim each corner point.

(See Fig. 2)

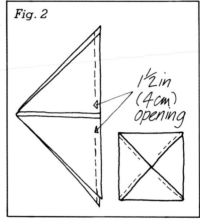

Fig. 2

1½ in (4cm) opening

Turn right side out through the opening, press, slipstitch the opening, then press the corners so they meet at the centre. These creases will be the seam lines.

(See Fig. 3)

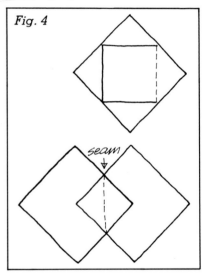

Fig. 3

Fold
Fold
Fold
Fold

To make a row: Place two squares seamless sides together, and stitch along one corner crease line. The beginning and end of the seam should be securely fastened by backstitching. When open, these two corners form a square on which a Window patch will be sewn. The number of squares in a row is determined by the size of the project.

(See Fig. 4)

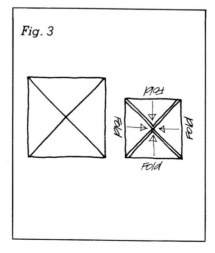

Fig. 4

seam

Stitching rows together: Place rows, seamless sides together, carefully matching all seams. Stitch along the crease line.

(See Fig. 5)

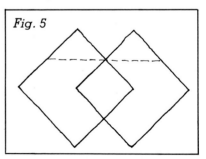

Fig. 5

Fig. 6

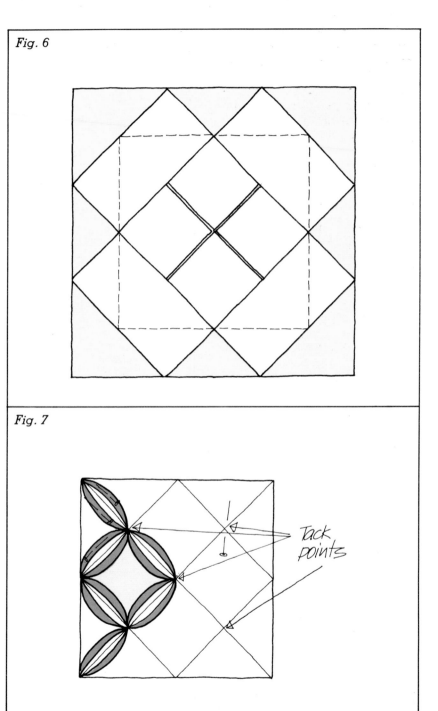

Attaching Windows to background: The centre of the prepared Windows is placed on the centre of the background fabric. Stitch along the crease lines.

(See Fig. 6)

Forming Points: Bring the four points to the centre of each square, and with small stitches, tack the four points together securely to the centre of the square.

Stitching Window patches: Pin the Window patches to the centre of the Window squares, with batting, if used, underneath. Bring the folded edges back over the raw edges of the Window patch and blindstitch in place, starting and ending ¼ inch (5 millimetres) from each end. This forms a secondary pattern. Keep adding patches until all have been stitched in postion. To complete the petal design on the outer folded edges where no patches have been added, continue to fold and blindstitch these edges.

(See Fig. 7)

Inserting a second colour to Window background: This is optional and should be done before bringing the four points to the centre. Cut a square of fabric ½ inch (13 millimetres) larger than the square formed by crease lines. Fold under ¼ inch (6 millimetres) on all four sides and blind stitch to centre of crease lined square, then proceed with stitching in the window patches.

(See Fig. 8)

Fig. 7

Fig. 8

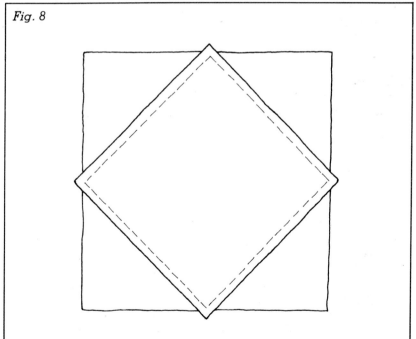

Tack points

To Make a Cushion

The cushion illustrated makes good use of an attractive glazed chintz fabric. The design was a very large one, but the smaller flowers were cut out for the Window patches and the border design used to surround the Cathedral Window block. The Windows were made of fine unbleached calico. The Cathedral Window block was made up of twelve 9 inch (23 centimetre) squares of unbleached calico, twelve 2½ inch (6.4 centimetre) squares of chintz and twelve 2 inch (5.2 centimetre) squares of a light batting. The batting is not essential but does add to the finished appearance of the cushion.

The Cathedral Window block was made up following the Construction Method (Page 64) then blindstitched onto the border design. Quarter inch (0.5 centimetre) cord was covered with the chintz fabric and attached to the front of the cushion.

A pillow case closing was used. The back was cut out of chintz, half the size of the front plus 4 inches (10 centimetres) for the overlap. It was then tacked to hold it firm until the front and back were sewn together using the machine zipper foot.

To Make an Apron

Materials

Print fabric: 1 yard (1 metre).
Unbleached calico for windows: ¾ yard (70 centimetres).
2 buttons.

The apron illustrated used the same printed fabric for the Window patches, but a contrasting fabric would look equally effective, in which case a further 10 inches (25 centimetres) of fabric would be required.

Cutting

Windows: cut eleven 9 inch (23 centimetre) squares of unbleached calico.
Window Patches: cut eleven 2½ inch (6.4 centimetre) squares of chosen print fabric.
Apron skirt: cut 30 x 21 inches (75 x 53 centimetres) of print.
Apron waistband: cut 18 x 3 inches (45 x 7.5 centimetres).
Apron ties: cut two 34 x 3 inches (85 x 7.5 centimetres) print.
Apron straps: cut two 27 inches (70 x 7.5 centimetres) print.

Cathedral Window

Following the construction method (Page 64), make up the bib block by making the rows of two, and the border block of one row of seven Windows. Both blocks are joined to the apron skirt before completing the Windows.

Open the points back on the bib block, and sew to the centre of the waistband, along crease lines.

(See Fig. 1)

Fold the wrong sides of the strap together and stitch, leaving one end open. Turn, slipstitch the open end, and attach a strap to each end of bib top ⅛ inch (3 millimetres) from the edge.

(See Fig. 2)

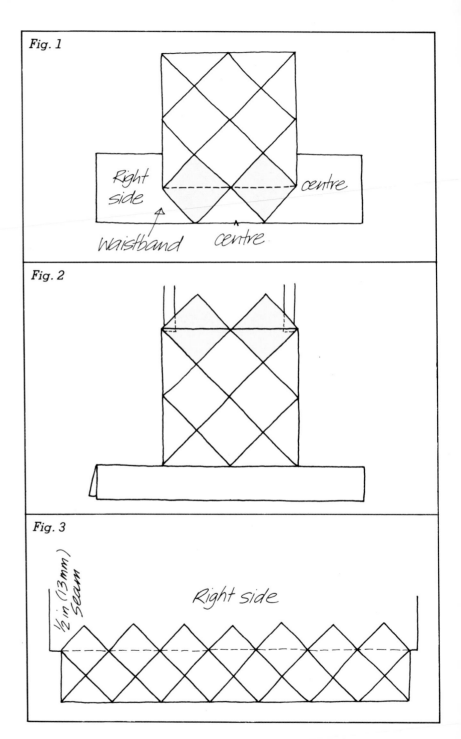

Fig. 1

Right side   centre

waistband   centre.

Fig. 2

Fig. 3

½ in (13mm) Seam

Right side

66

Attach the window patches, following General Instructions.

To attach the skirt block, open out the points and sew to the skirt along crease lines, ½ inch (13 millimetres) from the bottom of the skirt and ½ inch (13 millimetres) in from each side of the skirt. Turn under and slipstitch the raw edge of the bottom to the back of Windows. Hem the side edges of the skirt. Complete the border by attaching the remaining Window patches.

(See Fig. 3)

Stitch a tie to each end of waistband, right sides together.

(See Fig. 4)

Stitch along lengthways and ends, turn and topstitch.

(See Fig. 5)

Gather the top of the skirt to fit the waistband, and stitch it to the right side of the waistband. Turn under the raw edge of waistband, and slipstitch it closed.

Make a buttonhole on each end of the straps, cross the straps at the back and measure the position of buttons. Sew on the buttons.

(See Fig. 6)

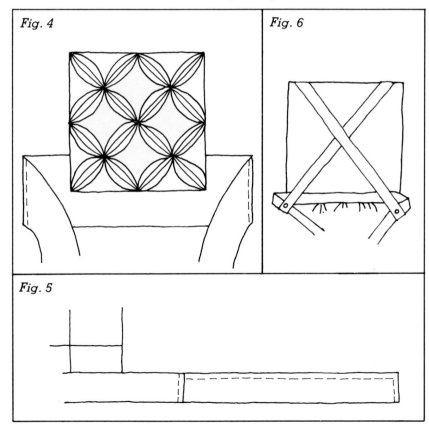

Fig. 4

Fig. 6

Fig. 5

Christmas Tree Ornament

Cutting: These are made from brightly coloured scraps of fabric. A ¼ inch (6 millimetre) seam is included in all the measurements. Cut three ½ inch (13 centimetre) squares from solid colour, three of the pattern given from dark print and three 1¼ inch (3.2 centimetre) squares of a light print.

(See Fig. 1)

Fig. 1

Cathedral Window Christmas Tree Ornament

Template same size

Cut 3

Follow the General Instructions (Page 64) as far as Fig. 2. Press the two opposite corners to the middle to mark the sewing line.

Starting and finishing ⅛ inch (3 millimetres) from each end, sew the three blocks together to make a ring, securing each end firmly.

(See Fig. 3)

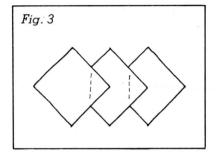

Fig. 3

Pin the dark print patch to the fronts. Fold the edges of the solid print down and slipstitch to make the window.

(See Fig. 4)

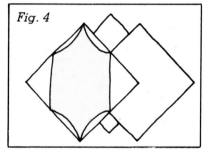

Fig. 4

Tack the points in the centre as shown.

(See Fig. 5)

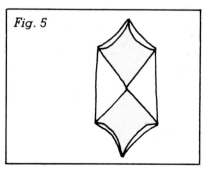

Fig. 5

Pin the small, light print patches as shown. Fold the edges of the solid print as for the dark print patches, and slipstich round all four sides of the small windows.

(See Fig. 6)

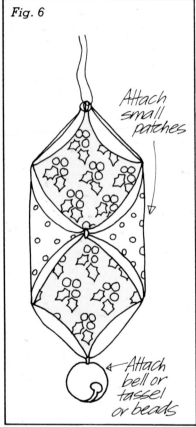

Fig. 6

Attach small patches

Attach bell or tassel or beads

Bring the three points together at the top, and sew firmly. Repeat for the bottom points. Attach gold or silver thread for hanging. The ornaments illustrated have a bell attached to the bottom, but a tassel or bright beads could be used instead. To make the ornaments really sparkle, sew on sequins to reflect the Christmas Tree lights.

Pincushion or Lavender Bag

Materials

Unbleached calico and scraps of any printed fabric. Filling of choice.

Cutting

For windows cut four 5 inch (13 centimetre) squares. For Window patches, cut eight 1¼ inch (3.2 centimetre) squares.

Making

Prepare the four 5 inch (13 centimetre) squares as far as Fig. 3 in the General Instructions (Page 64). Join the four points at the centre as shown.

(See Fig. 4)

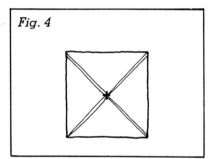

Fig. 4

Topstitch two sets of two together.

(See Fig. 5)

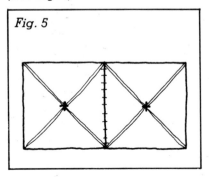

Fig. 5

Join these two sets together along the long sides.

(See Fig. 6)

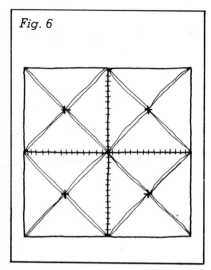

Fig. 6

Refold the block so the ends are now in the centre. Join the opening as far as the centre, leaving the remainder open to insert the filling.

(See Fig. 7)

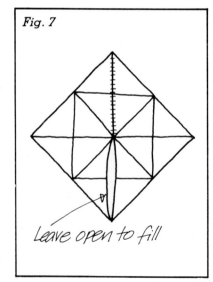

Fig. 7

Leave open to fill

Attach seven of the patches to the windows, fill with fibrefill or lavender, slipstitch the opening, then attach the remaining eighth patch.

(See Fig. 8)

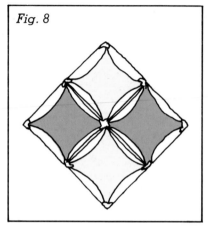

Fig. 8

Using a strong thread, take a few tacks right through the centre to the other side and back again; pull tightly and fasten off securely. A fancy button or a small ribbon bow may be attached to the centre as a finishing touch.

Seminole Patchwork

Seminole patchwork is a form of strip-piecing in which long strips of fabric are sewn together to form multicoloured bands which are cut into segments, arranged to form geometric designs, then sewn again, resulting in a patterned band which can then be incorporated into clothing or other items.

This technique was used by the Seminole and Miccosukee Indians in Florida, although not exclusively, as early colonists also worked with strip piecing. However, the Indian work was distinctive with its clear, bright colours and intricate designs. The bands of fabric were joined together, interspersed with plain fabrics, to create a fabric from which the pieces for a garment were cut. The resulting garments with their many intricately patterned horizontal bands of patchwork in brilliant colours, characterised the Seminole clothing from around 1910. They are still made today, partly for the tourist market.

Although the technique appears to be very difficult because the more intricate designs may have thousands of tiny pieces, the method used to construct the bands is in fact quite straightforward, as none of the small fragments are handled individually. Once the basic method has been mastered, there are endless possibilities for design variations. Those with a creative bent will enjoy experimenting with their own ideas.

Construction

Strips of coloured fabric are sewn together to form a band.

(See Fig. 1)

The band is cut into segments, either straight or angled, depending on the pattern desired.

(See Fig. 2)

The segments are arranged in an offset manner and sewn together.

(See Fig. 3)

Edging strips are sewn along the long edges of the band to provide a finished edge. The band is now ready to be incorporated into your project.

(See Fig. 4)

The effect of Seminole patchwork depends to a large extent on very accurate sewing and cutting. The following guidelines will help you to achieve this.

Cutting and Marking the Fabric

It is preferable to cut the strips on the lengthways grain of the fabric, as this minimises the stretch. If you do not have sufficient fabric, the crossways grain can be used. Cutting can be simplified by folding the fabric carefully in four, and cutting through all four thicknesses.

Mark the fabric with a fine black ball-point pen and cut the required number of strips. Using a clear plastic ruler or set of strip templates in conjunction with a rotary cutter will make cutting the strips a breeze.

Sewing the Bands

Some patterns require a strip which has a finished width of ¼ inch (6 millimetres). With such a narrow strip, the least variation will detract from the finished appearance. This difficulty can be overcome by sewing the first seam as usual, then sewing the second seam using the first seam instead of the cut edge as your guide. The finished strip will be exactly ¼ inch (6 millimetres) wide with any inaccuracies confined to within the seam allowance.

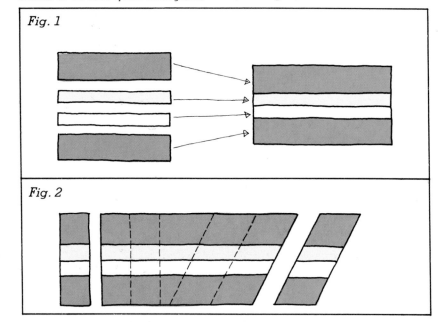

Fig. 1

Fig. 2

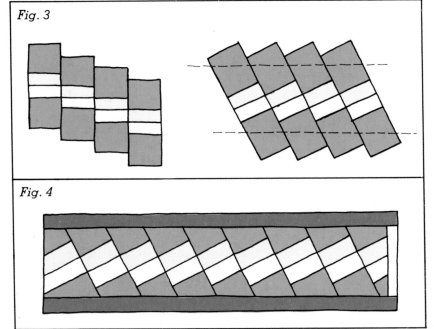

Fig. 3

Fig. 4

Ironing the Bands

When the strips have been sewn into a band, this must be pressed before it is cut into segments. Press all the seam allowances in the same direction, then press from the right side to make sure there are no folds beside the seam lines.

Marking and Cutting the Segments

Mark a perpendicular line at the left end of the band. For straight segments, mark the desired width with lines parallel to the initial line. Cut the band along these lines.

(See Fig. 5)

For angled segments, mark along the top and bottom edges of the band at the distances indicated on the pattern, and draw lines connecting the marks. These lines form the cutting lines.

(See Fig. 6)

Construction of Seminole Band for Bag Pocket

Rust: 30 x 4½ inches (75 x 11.5 centimetres).
Brown: 30 x 3½ inches (75 x 9 centimetres).
Beige: 30 x 4½ inches (75 x 11.5 centimetres).

Join strips into a band with the brown strip in the centre. (Strip widths include a ¼ inch (6 millimetre) seam allowance). Press seams down.

Mark and cut the band into straight segments 3½ inches (9 centimetres) wide.

(See Fig. 7)

Turn alternate pieces upside down. Join segments so the bottom seam line of brown strip meets the top seam line of brown strip in the adjacent segment.

(See Fig. 8)

Press the band. Mark a line 10 inches (25 centimetres) away from the points of the brown squares, along both edges of band.

(See Fig. 9)

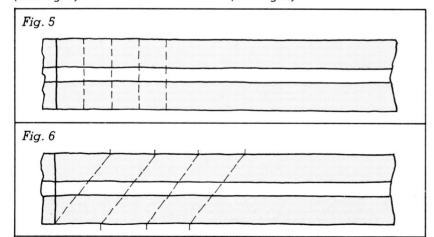

Fig. 5

Fig. 6

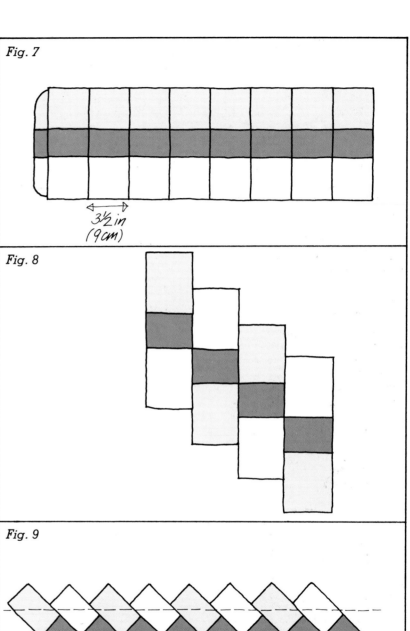

Fig. 7

3½ in (9cm)

Fig. 8

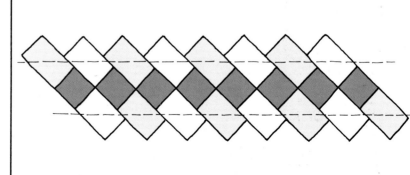

Fig. 9

Cut strips 12 inches (30 centimetres) wide from beige fabric, and place them on the band, right sides together. Align cut edge of strip with the line drawn on top edge of band. Sew with a ¼ inch (6 millimetre) seam. Sew a beige strip to the bottom of the band in the same way. Trim the excess off the band, level with the beige strip. Add a 12 inch (30 centimetre) rust strip to the bottom edge of the panel, and a 24 inch (60 centimetre) strip to the top edge. Cut the panel to the same width as the front of the bag (18 inches or 45 centimetres), press, and baste a piece of lining fabric to the wrong side of the patchwork panel, which is now ready for use as the front pocket of the bag.

(See Fig. 10)

Materials

Polyester cotton canvas: 27 x 42 inches (70 x 106 centimetres).

Two 15 inch (38 centimetre) lengths of ½ inch (12 millimetre) dowel rod. 4½ yards (4 metres) of cotton webbing 1 inch (2.5 centimetres) wide. Thread to match webbing. ¼ inch (6 millimetre) particle board: 4 x 16 inches (10 x 40 centimetres).

Construction

Mark the canvas according to the dimensions given in Fig. 11. Cut out the bag.

(See Fig. 11)

Cut out handle grip from the top edges of front and back. Bind edges with webbing; attach webbing by folding it in half to enclose raw edge, and stitch with a wide zig-zag stitch, making sure the underside is caught by the stitching. Bind the top edge of the patchwork pocket and the short edges of the gusset.
Form the casing for the handles

by turning under 1¼ inches (3 centimetres) either side of the handle grip. Stitch down securely.

Turn under ⅜ inch (1 centimetre) at each end of base lining and stitch. Place base lining on gusset, wrong sides together with the centres of

each piece aligned. Stitch through all thicknesses at one end of the base lining. Machine baste long edges together.

(See Fig. 12)

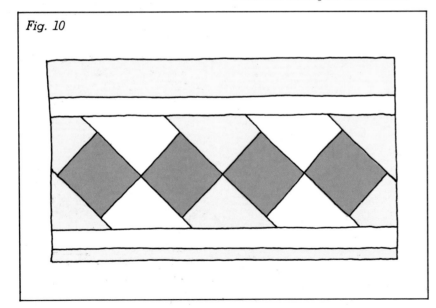

Fig. 10

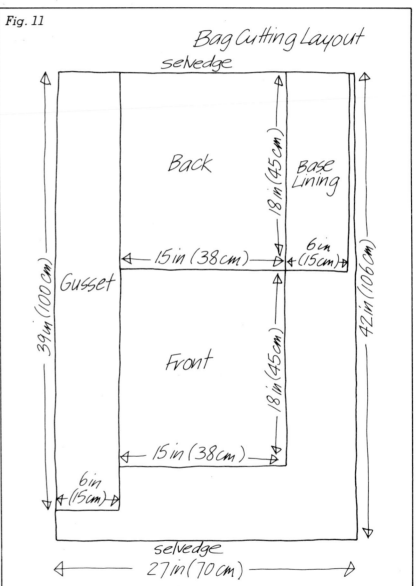

Fig. 11

Bag Cutting Layout

selvedge

Back

Gusset

Front

Base Lining

39 in (100 cm)

42 in (106 cm)

18 in (45 cm)

18 in (45 cm)

6 in (15 cm)

15 in (38 cm)

15 in (38 cm)

6 in (15 cm)

selvedge

27 in (70 cm)

Machine baste the patchwork panel to the front.

Join the bag sections together as follows: With wrong sides together, pin the front to the gusset, matching centres. Stitch across lower edge with a ½ inch (12 millimetre) seam, beginning and ending the seam ½ inch (12 millimetres) from the side edge. Join the back to the gusset in the same way.

(See Fig. 13)

Clip the seam allowance of the gusset almost to the stitching, then pin gusset to side edges as shown and stitch the side seams. The gusset should end just below the handle casing.

(See Fig. 15)

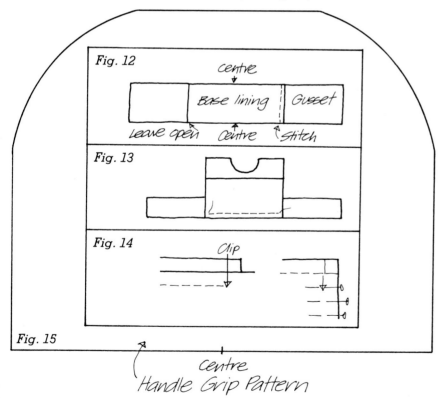

Fig. 12
centre
Base lining   Gusset
Leave open   Centre   Stitch

Fig. 13

Fig. 14
Clip

Fig. 15

Centre
Handle Grip Pattern

(See Fig. 14)

Trim the seam to ¼ inch (6 millimetres), rounding the bottom corners. Enclose the seams with cotton webbing, beginning the stitching at the top edge of one side, but stopping just below the handle casing on the other side. Leave 4 inches (10 centimetres) of webbing extending at the top. Insert the dowel handles, then finish stitching the webbing, either by hand or machine. Turn the bag inside out, and insert the base support.

Attach a press stud or Velcro handy dot to the upper edge of the pocket to hold it closed.

Seminole Bordered Skirt

This skirt was made using Vogue pattern 1080, which is particularly suitable as it has a band around the lower edge. A 6 inch (15 centimetre) strip of skirt fabric was sewn along the lower edge of the Seminole band, and the lower band pattern piece of the skirt was cut from this, omitting one side seam. The skirt was then made up following the pattern instructions.

Any skirt pattern which has fairly straight side edges, with the fullness gathered or pleated into the waistband, would be equally suitable. Avoid patterns which are flared, as the patchwork band has straight ends, and will not accommodate the flare of the skirt. Also avoid gored patterns, as unnecessary joins in the patchwork will detract from the appearance.

Construction of the Seminole Band

Following the basic method and using the colours of your choice, cut strips of fabrics A and B. You will require two strips of A, each

60 x ¾ inch (150 x 2 centimetres) and one strip of B 60 x 1 inch (150 x 2.5 centimetres). To obtain the length required, the strips will have to be joined, but when the strip is cut into segments, those with a join can be discarded. Join the strips to form a band as shown. Cut into 1 inch (2.5 centimetre) segments.

(See Fig. 1)

Cut two lengths of C 60 x 1¾ inches (150 x 4.5 centimetres). Cut two lengths of A 60 x ¾ inch (150 x 2 centimetres). Join to form two bands.

(See Fig. 2)

Turn the AB segments sideways and insert them between the two AC bands. Stitch so the AB segments are just touching.

(See Fig. 3)

Press the band, and cut into 1½ inch (4 centimetre) segments.

(See Fig. 4)

73

Offset the segments so the lower seamline of A meets the upper seamline of A in the adjacent segment. Join the segments (save time by chainsewing), and press the band.

(See Fig. 5)

Mark a line on the right side ¼ inch (6 millimetres) above and below the points of A. The design must be centred between these lines which are used as a guide for attaching edging strips. This skirt has two edging strips, one of B, 1⅜ inches (3.5 centimetres) wide, and one of C, ¾ inch (2 centimetres) wide.

(See Fig. 6)

Back the band with lining fabric, and it is ready to use in your skirt.

(See Fig. 7)

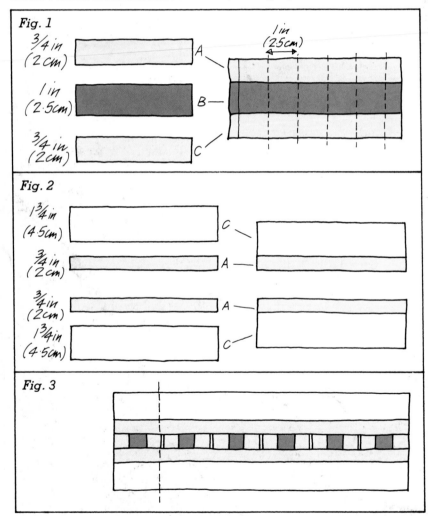

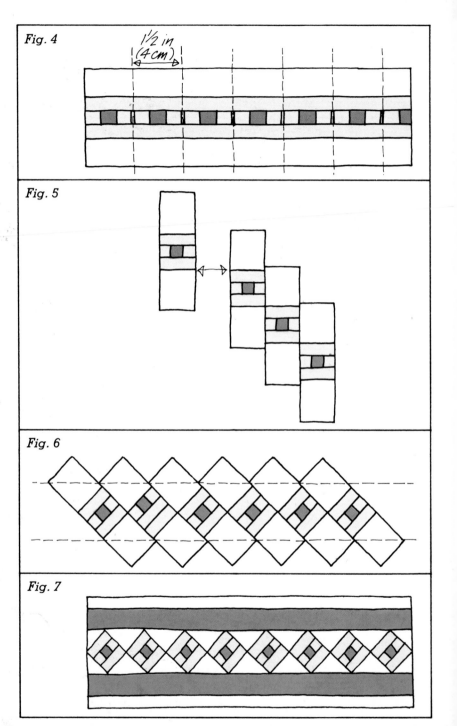

Folded Star

This is a very simple and effective technique. The choice of colours is important in order to show the star design. Choose a light and dark print fabric, or perhaps a solid and a print fabric. As in all other patchwork, wash and iron the fabrics before use.

Once the basic technique has been mastered, the star can be incorporated in many projects.

At least three rows of triangles must be used, but additional rows may be added as shown in the table mats and appliance covers, photographed on Pages 75, 78.

Circles are used if the rows are ½ inch (13 millimetres) or less apart. If the rows are to be placed further apart use squares as this will allow more fabric at the outer corners to cover the raw edges of the previous row.

Green Table Mat

Materials

Fabrics: 16 inches (40 centimetres) of each.
Firm interfacing: One 10 inch (26 centimetre) diameter circle.
Backing: One 10 inch (26 centimetre) diameter circle of calico.
Batting: One 10 inch (26 centimetre) diameter circle.
Bias Binding: 1 yard (1 metre).
Cutting: For the centre row, five 5 inch (13 centimetre) diameter circles.
For the next three rows, cut eight 5 inch (13 centimetre) circles of each colour.

For the fifth outside row, cut eight 6½ inch (17 centimetre) diameter circles. Prepare the interfacing as shown in Fig. 1. Fold the circle in half, then quarters and eighths, open out the circle and rule the fold marks in pencil. These guide lines will not show on the finished article, so make sure they are quite clear.

(See Fig. 1)

For the next step, it is a good idea to lower the ironing board and sit down, as there is quite a lot of pressing required.

Fold each circle in half and press.

(See Fig. 2,3)

To make the triangle, bring points X and Y to centre and press.

Open out one of the middle circles and place it on the interfacing, lining up the fold lines with the pencilled lines. Place the remaining four triangles with the points meeting in the centre, lining up the pencilled guide lines. Tack the points together through all thicknesses. Tack the outer edge in place. This can be done by machine. Pin to hold the folds in place and use a large stitch.

(See Fig. 4)

One by one, place the eight triangles of the next row ½ inch (13 millimetres) from the centre, being careful to line up with the pencilled lines; tack through all layers at the points. Tack the outer edge in place as in the previous row. Be careful to overlap all the triangles in the same direction.

(See Fig. 5)

Repeat this step for the remaining three rows, remembering to keep within the guide lines.

(See Fig. 6,7)

Pin, and tack together the star, batting and backing. Sew the binding to the front and slipstitch to the wrong side.

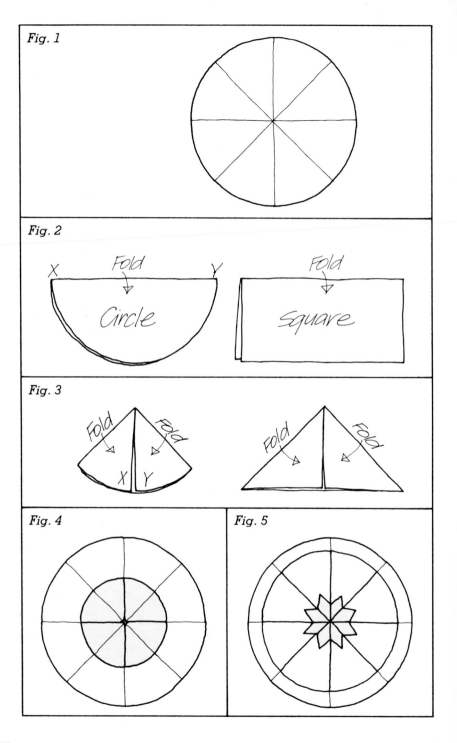

Fig. 1

Fig. 2

X Fold Y
Circle

Fold
Square

Fig. 3

Fold Fold
X Y

Fold Fold

Fig. 4

Fig. 5

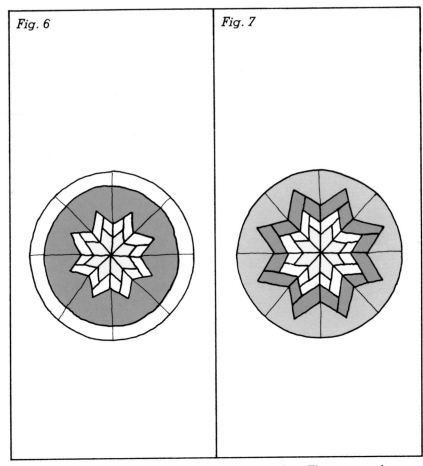

Fig. 6

Fig. 7

Brown Table Mat

Materials

Fabric used: 16 inches (40 centimetres) of each.
Firm interfacing: One 11 inch (28 centimetre) diameter circle.
Backing: One 11 inch (28 centimetre) diameter circle of calico.
Bias binding: 1 yard (1 metre).

Follow the instructions for the Green Table Mat up to and including Row Three.

To change the shape of the star, the outer rows can be increased to 16 triangles. These triangles can be the same colour or eight each of two different fabrics.

Row 4: tack the point of a triangle to each star point of the previous row tacking the outer edge.

(See Fig. 8)

Row 5: tack the remaining eight triangles to each centre fold of the previous row.

(See Fig. 9)

Finish and bind as for the Green Mat (Page 76).

Tea Cosy

Materials

Two pieces of main fabric: 10 x 12 inches (25 x 31 centimetres).
Star fabric: 16 inches (40 centimetres of all colours.
One 7½ inch (19 centimetre) diameter circle of interfacing to back the star.
Batting: 16 inches (40 centimetres).
One 9 inch (23 centimetre) square of light interfacing or lining to make the window for the star.
Two pieces of lining 10 x 12 inches (25 x 31 centimetres).
Bias binding: 1 yard (1 metre).

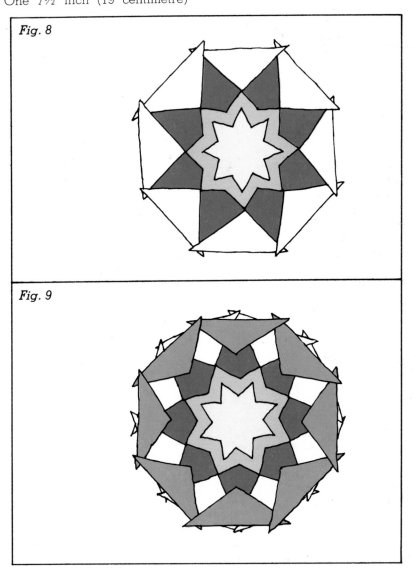

Fig. 8

Fig. 9

Follow the directions for the Green table mat to make a 7½ inch (19 centimetre) diameter star using 5 inch (13 centimetre) diameter circles placed ½ inch (13 millimetres) apart.

Cut the main fabric, batting and lining to shape. Oversew the batting to the lining on the front and back.

Using the 9 inch (23 centimetre) square of interfacing or lining, make a window on the front piece of main material and insert completed star.

Making the Window

Cut a square of fabric 2 inches (5 centimetres) larger than the diameter of the finished star for facing. On the wrong side, draw a circle the size of the finished star.

Right sides centre facing on the front of the cosy. Sew along the marked line. Cut out the centre leaving a ¼ inch (6 millimetre) seam allowance. Clip seam allowance. Turn the facing to the inside and press. Place the star behind the window, centring it carefully.

Lift the top fabric and tack the star to facing and sew round close to previous seam. This stitching will not show on the front.

To Assemble

Place the prepared lining to the wrong sides of back and front with batting in the middle. Tack right round the edges. Pin and sew bias binding to the bottom edge of the cosy, right sides together. Fold the binding to the back over the raw edge; slipstitch down. Repeat on the second side.

Pin the two halves of the cosy together, and tack round the sides and top. Pin and sew bias binding along the sides and top to within ¼ inch (6 millimetres) of bottom, turn in ¼ inch (6 millimetre) seam on the

binding and sew. Fold binding. Fold the binding to the other side and slipstitch down.

Appliance Covers

Appliance covers vary so much in size that it is not possible to give exact measurements. Both covers shown in the photograph were made the same way.

Measure the length, breadth and depth of the appliance, and cut two pieces measuring the length by the breadth plus ½ inch (12 millimetres) which allows a ¼ inch (6 millimetre) seam for the front and back. For the gusset, cut one piece measuring the length plus breadth plus ½ inch (12 millimetres), by the depth of the appliance plus ½ inch (12 millimetres).

If a fairly firm fabric is used, it is only necessary to line the front. However, if a lightweight fabric is used, the appearance of the covers will be improved by the addition of a light needled polyester placed between the lining and the outer material.

Materials

Two yards (1.70 metres) should be sufficient of the main fabric to make both covers, but check against measurements of the appliance to be covered.

Star Fabric

16 inches (40 centimetres) of each fabric used for each star.

One 9 inch (23 centimetre) diameter circle of firm interfacing for each star.

One 9 inch (23 centimetre) square of needled polyester wadding to back each completed star.

More will be required if it is going to be used to back the gusset and back of covers.

Lining.

Bias binding.

Construction

Make the star as for Green table mat up to Row 5 (Page 76). For Row 6 use eight 6½ inch (17 centimetre) squares.

Tack the needled polyester wadding to the back of the star; tack the star to the lining.

Using a square of main fabric, make a window on the front of the cover, following the directions given. Stitch the star on the lining into the window. This stitching will show on the lining. Tack the lining to the front around the edges.

With the wrong sides together, sew the gusset to the front so the seam is on the right side. Sew the gusset to the back in the same way. Trim the seam to ⅛ inch (3 millimetres).

Sew on the bias to back and front gusset seams, then sew bias along the bottom edge.

If the cover is to be lined, cut out two pieces of lining the same size as the front and back, and one piece of lining the same size as the gusset. Also cut the same size pieces in the needled polyester wadding. Place the needled polyester wadding between the lining and the outer fabric, pin and tack together.

With the wrong sides together, sew the gusset to the front so the seam is on the right side. Sew the gusset to the back in the same way. Trim the seam to ⅛ inch (3 millimetres) and bind around as instructed above.

Crazy Patchwork

Crazy patchwork, also known as Victorian patchwork and Random patchwork, was very popular in the late 1800s. Its origins, like most other patchwork, can be traced back to the sheer economic necessity of making something out of nothing as quickly as possible.

The essential economy of crazy patchwork lay in the fact that it was possible to include many different kinds of materials in the one quilt. The scraps of fabric could be any shape, which meant that every remnant could be used, and as they were sewn onto a foundation, this helped to prolong the life of fabrics that had already seen a lot of wear.

Gradually, however, the rough homespun materials gave way to the delicate silks, satin brocades and velvets so beloved by the Victorians. These quilts were then embellished with lace and ribbons and most beautifully embroidered and could indeed be described as fabric collages, reaching the pinnacle of sheer luxury — or monumental bad taste — depending on the particular example. Undoubtedly the makers would have shared the same pride of achievement whatever anyone else thought of the results.

The construction of crazy patchwork does not require great skill in the stitching or planning of a piece of work. Now, as in the past, any kind of fabric may be used, and almost invariably the pieces are those found in the dressmaker's rag-bag.

However, it is well to remember the basic rules about fabrics, if the project is something that will have to be washed. Fabrics should be pre-washed to check for shrinkage and colour fastness. They should also be of similar weights. If the chosen project is something like a bag it will no doubt be made to match a particular colour scheme, which must be borne in mind when sorting out the materials to be used. Choose fabrics that look well together.

The nice thing about crazy patchwork is that you can see how a particular patch is fitting in before you actually sew it down.

Preparation of the patches is very simple; any shaped piece of fabric can be used. Cut off the frayed edges and any very irregular bits. With a pile of patches trimmed and prepared, the idea is to arrange them on to a foundation that is not too stiff. Each patch is then laid on to the foundation with the raw edges over- or under-lapping those of the next patches by about ⅝ inch (1.5 centimetres).

It is convenient to start off in a top corner, but the first patch can be placed anywhere on the foundation. Pin this patch down, then place the second patch to overlap the raw edge of the first patch on one side, turning under a ¼ inch (1 centimetre) hem on the overlapping edge.

(See Fig. 1,2)

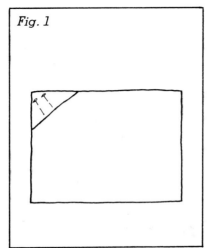

Fig. 1

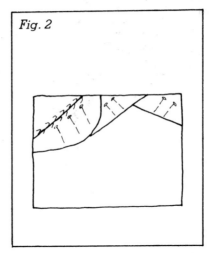

Fig. 2

At this point you must decide whether you can manage by just pinning your patches down and not getting the sewing thread too tangled up in pins, or if you will find it easier to tack the patches before sewing, removing the tacking threads later.

Although reference is made to crazy patchwork quilts, in fact, originally they were not padded, usually having been made from rough homespun woollen fabric which was very warm. If an extra layer was used, it was tied to the top and not quilted.

Today we do use batting for quilts, or a lightweight needle-punch for small projects such as bags or placemats. This is placed between the patches and the foundation material and the embroidery stitches perform the double function of sewing down the patches and quilting at the same time. Use any embroidery stitch that spans both sides of the seam. Feather stitch or herringbone are both suitable, but here is an ideal opportunity to show off what excellent embroidery you can do by using a variety of stitches. Any embroidery or quilting thread can be used, the weight of the thread will depend on how much you want the embroidery to show up.

Contemporary crazy patchwork is very often machine sewn. It is possible to proceed in the same manner as the hand sewn method, but using either a zig-zag stitch or just straight sewing. The seams can then be embroidered, or you can just embroider around any particular patches you want to emphasise.

A third method is somewhat similar to strip quilting and is also machine sewn. The foundation fabric and a light batting are tacked together around the edges. With the batting side up, pin the first patch anywhere.

(See Fig. 3)

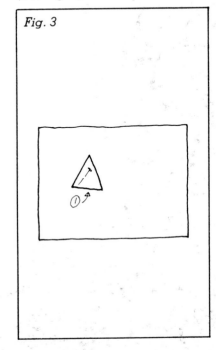

Fig. 3

Lay the next piece right side down, on top of the first one, with the edges together, and sew through all thicknesses.

(See Fig. 4)

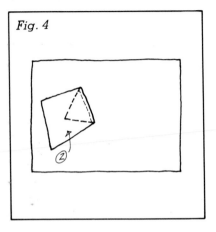

Fig. 4

Open the second patch to the right side and trim to whatever shape is desired.

(See Fig. 5)

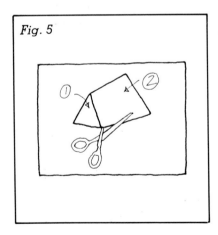

Fig. 5

Pin this second patch until the third patch is sewn and trimmed. Continue in the same way until the foundation is covered.

It will be easier to handsew any curved edges. Turn under and pin these hems, and handsew them later when the machine sewing is completed. Try not to leave awkward angles to fill up by being careful not to extend a new patch beyond the end of the one it is being sewn on to. If this does happen, a simple solution is to overlap the protruding bit with a new patch.

It is not really necessary to embroider this kind of project using this method, unless you wish to, as it will already have a quilted effect.

Crazy patchwork technique, using any of the three methods given, can be very readily adapted to quilt making using blocks of foundation fabric cut in 12 to 18 inch (30 to 45 centimetre) squares. Complete the blocks, lay them out to determine how they look best, sew them together in rows, then join the rows together, being careful to match the seams.

Cut the backing material a little larger than the top and as the top is already quilted, it is advisable to tie the two together. Tack the top to the backing, lay them face down, and mark every 4 inches (10 centimetres) as a guide to the ties. Use a long needle, threaded with quilting or embroidery thread. Push the needle straight down through all layers, leaving about 2 inches (5 centimetres) of thread on the top, and come right back up to the surface about ¼ inch (6 millimetres) away. Tie a square knot and trim the threads to about 1 inch (2.5 centimetres).

Continue in the same manner until all the quilt is tied.

For the binding, choose a

fabric that looks well with the quilt, and bind around.

To Make the Crazy Patchwork Bag

Materials

Scraps of material for the patches.
Unbleached calico for the foundation.
Batting (this is optional, but was used in the bag illustrated).
Quilting or embroidery thread.
2 wooden handles.
Soft rope for handles: 1 yard (1 metre).
Toning material for top and lining: 1 yard (1 metre).

Cutting

Cut two rectangles of the unbleached calico 14 x 10½ inches (36 x 27) and one gusset 32 x 3½ inches (82 x 9) centimetres for foundation.

Batting (optional)

Two rectangles 14 x 10½ inches (36 x 27 centimetres) and one gusset 32 x 3½ inches (82 x 9 centimetres).

Lining and Top

Cut two rectangles 14 x 10½ inches (36 x 27 centimetres) and one gusset 32 x 3½ inches (82 x 9 centimetres).

Pocket and Tops

One rectangle 8 x 5 inches (20 x 12 centimetres) for the pocket and for the tops cut two rectangles 15 x 7 inches (38 x 18 centimetres).
Elastic for top of pocket.

Prepare the foundation using any of the three methods described. The bag photographed used

the first method, and the patches were sewn down using feather stitch. The bag was assembled by machine.

To assemble

Join the gusset to the front, starting and ending 1½ inches (4 centimetres) from the top. Repeat with the back.

(See Fig. 6)

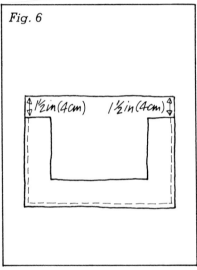

Fig. 6

1½in(4cm)   1½in(4cm)

Lining

Hem across the top of the pocket and insert the elastic. Press under a ¼ inch (6 millimetre seam) allowance on the other three sides, and sew to one side of the lining. Join the lining pieces together as for the outer bag.

Now, with the right side of the lining to the right side of the bag, sew down the 1½ inches (4 centimetres) from the top, across the gusset and up the 1½ inches (4 centimetres) to the top on the other side. Repeat with second side.

(See Fig. 7)

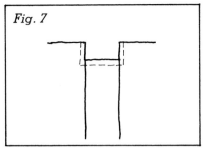

Fig. 7

Turn lining to the inside, and topstitch round the seams just completed. Tack raw edges of lining and bag together at the top.

Take the two 15 x 7 inch (38 x 18 centimetre) rectangles, and press under a ¼ inch (6 millimetre) seam on one long side of each.

(See Fig. 8)

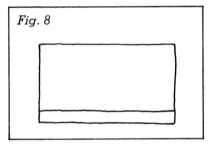

Fig. 8

Pin and sew the unpressed side to the top of the bag, with right side of the top to the lining. There will be an overlap which should be hemmed back.

(See Fig. 9)

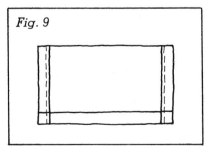

Fig. 9

Bring the pressed side of the top to the front and topstitch down. Sew a parallel line of stitching, approximately 1½ inches (4 centimetres) away, to form a tunnel for the wooden handles. It is wise to pin this first and check the thickness of the dowelling in the handles before sewing. Repeat with second side.

(See Fig. 10)

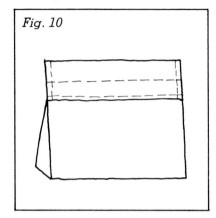

Fig. 10

Cut the rope in two, knot all four ends, leaving 1¼ inches (3 centimetres) at each end to unravel. Sew firmly to the top on the seam line, 3 inches (8 centimetres) from each end. Insert the wooden handles in the tunnels.

Jewellery Roll

Materials

Scraps of material for patches.
Rectangle of 8½ x 13 inches (22 x 33 centimetres) of unbleached calico for the Foundation.
Taffeta for lining: 30 inches (75 centimetres).
Light batting or needlepunch.
Gold embroidery thread.
Bias binding: 1½ yards (1.3 metres).
1 patent fastener for ring bar.

Cutting

Shape the unbleached calico and the batting by rounding off the corners. Cut one piece of lining the same size as the foundation.
Pockets: For the large pocket, cut 8½ x 7 inches (22 x 18 centimetres). Finished size 8½ x 6½ inches (22 x 16 centimetres).
Middle Pocket: Cut 8½ x 4½ inches (22 x 11 centimetres). Finished size 8½ x 3 inches (22 x 8 centimetres).
Top Pocket: Cut 8½ x 3¼ inches (22 x 8.5 centimetres). Finished size 8½ x 2¼ inches (22 x 5.5 centimetres).
Flaps: For the large pocket cut 8½ x 4 inches (22 x 10 centimetres). Finished size 8½ x 1¾ inches (22 x 4.5 centimetres).
Middle Pocket: Cut 8½ x 4 inches (22 x 10 centimetres). Finished size 8½ x 1¾ inches (22 x 4.5 centimetres).
Top Pocket: Cut 8½ x 4½ inches (22 x 11 centimetres). Finished size 8½ x 2¼ (22 x 5.5 centimetres).
Ring Bar: Cut a piece of lining 8¼ x 2¼ inches (21 x 5.5 centimetres). Finished size 7 x ½ inch (18 x 1.5 centimetres). Cut a piece of batting or needlepunch 7 x ½ inch (18 x 1.5 centimetres).

Prepare the top by placing the batting on the foundation, then sew on the patches using any of the three methods described. The jewellery roll shown was made using the first method and embroidered in feather stitch, using gold embroidery thread.

Lining

Hem the tops of all three pockets by folding down ½ inch (1 centimetre) twice, and use a decorative stitch to sew.

Flaps

Fold in two, right sides together, and stitch the short sides, shaping the seam to fit the curve of the foundation.

(See Fig. 11)

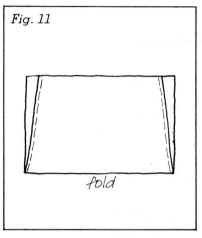

Fig. 11

fold

Trim, turn to the right side, press and topstitch as for the top of the pockets round three sides. Overcast the raw edge to neaten.

(See Fig. 12)

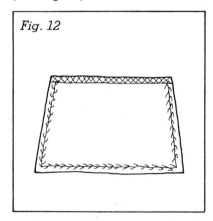

Fig. 12

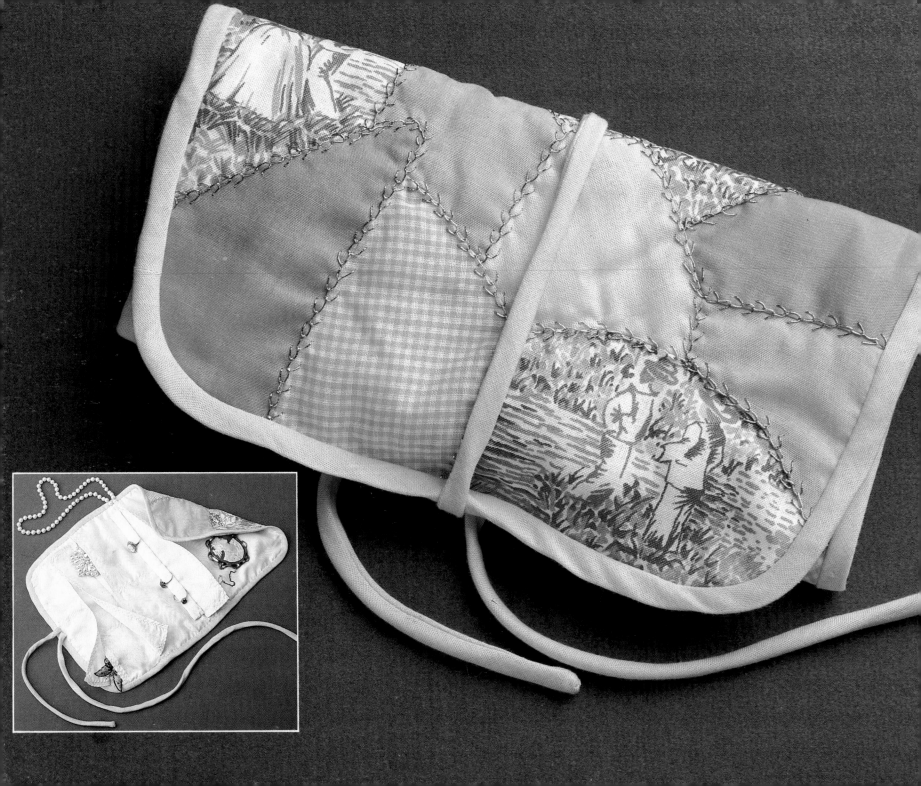

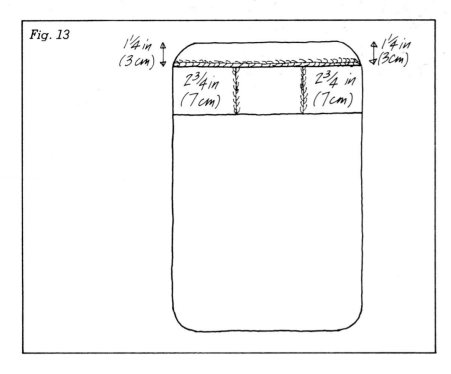

Fig. 13

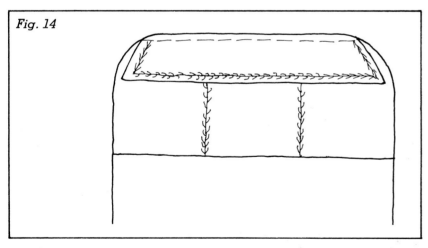

Fig. 14

Position and pin the top pocket to the shaped lining piece 1¼ inches (3 centimetres) from the top edge; trim to fit the curve, and tack at the edges. Sew down 2¾ inches (7 centimetres) from each edge to divide the pocket into three, using a decorative stitch.

(See Fig. 13)

Pin and tack the deepest flap to the top as shown.

(See Fig. 14)

Middle Pocket

Place the raw edge of the second flap to the lower edge of the top pocket and sew through all thicknesses. Neaten with a zig-zag stitch.

Place the top edge of the middle pocket over this line of stitching and sew down the middle to form two pockets. Use the same decorative stitch. Tack both sides. Press the flap down over the pocket.

Lower Pocket and Flap

Attach in the same way as the middle pocket, cutting off the corners to fit the rounded shape.

Ring Bar

Press a ¼ inch (6 millimetre) seam along one long side of the material; roll the piece of needlepunch or batting from the raw edge to the pressed edge and slipstitch it in place. Turn under and neaten both ends. Position it just above the flap of the lower pocket and sew firmly at one end. Attach the fastener to the other end.

To Assemble

Pin the pocketed lining to the prepared top piece, wrong sides together, and tack all round, trimming to fit if necessary.

To make the ties, cut two pieces of bias binding, one 18 inches (45 centimetres) and the other 9 inches (23 centimetres), whip the folded edges together and tack to the centre of the top outside edge.

Bind all round the edge, catching in the ties.

About the Authors

Peigi Martin

Susan Young

Born in Carrickfergus, Northern Ireland, Peigi Martin went to school in Belfast.

Peigi was introduced to patchwork by her sister-in-law who gave her two cardboard templates and some scraps of material. She hasn't stopped patchworking since.

Susan Young now lives in Devonport, Auckland, with husband and one son, Jeremy. Introduced to patchwork by her embroidery teacher, her initial interest has developed into a passion and an almost full-time occupation, making quilts and other articles for family and friends.

Further Reading

Bishop, Robert, and Safanda, Elizabeth. **A Gallery of Amish Quilts.** E. P. Dutton & Co., 1976.

Finlay, Ruth. **Old Patchwork Quilts and the Women Who Made Them.** J. B. Lippincott and Co., 1929.

Hinson, Dolores. **American Graphic Quilt Design.** Arco, New York, 1983.

Holstein, Jonathan. **The Pieced Quilt — an American Design Tradition.** New York Graphic Society, 1973.

McKendry, Ruth. **Traditional Quilts & Bedcoverings.** Van Nostrand Reinhold, New York, 1979.

Orlofsky, Patsy, and Orlofsky, Myron. **Quilts in America.** McGraw Hill Book Company, 1974.

Safford, Carleton L., and Bishop, Robert. **America's Quilts and Coverlets.** E. P. Dutton and Co., 1972.

Index